Excel® Quick and Easy

Michael Alexander

Dick Kusleika

WILEY

Adapted from Microsoft Excel 365 Bible, 2nd Edition, copyright 2025, John Wiley & Sons. Inc.

Published by John Wiley & Sons, Inc., Hoboken, New Jersey.

Published simultaneously in Canada and the United Kingdom.

ISBNs: 9781394345267 (paperback), 9781394345281 (ePDF), 9781394345274 (ePub)

For general information on our other products and services or for technical support, please contact our Customer Care Department within the United States at (800) 762-2974, outside the United States at (317) 572-3993 or fax (317) 572-4002. For product technical support, you can find answers to frequently asked questions or reach us via live chat at https://support.wiley.com.

If you believe you've found a mistake in this book, please bring it to our attention by emailing our Reader Support team at wileysupport@wiley.com with the subject line "Possible Book Errata Submission."

Wiley also publishes its books in a variety of electronic formats. Some content that appears in print may not be available in electronic formats. For more information about Wiley products, visit our web site at www.wiley.com.

Library of Congress Control Number: 2025934521

Cover images: © 200degrees/Getty Images, © Oleksandr Hruts/Getty Images

Cover design: Wiley

SKY10101153_032625

Contents

Contents

Introducing Excel

IN THIS CHAPTER

- Understanding what Excel is used for
- Learning the parts of an Excel window
- Moving around a worksheet

This chapter is an introductory overview of Excel 365. Excel 365 runs on Windows, macOS, the web, iOS, iPadOS, and Android, though not all functions are available outside of Windows and macOS. If you're already familiar with a previous version of Excel, reading (or at least skimming) this chapter is still a good idea.

Understanding What Excel Is Used For

Excel is the world's most widely used spreadsheet software and is part of the Microsoft Office suite. Other spreadsheet software is available, but Excel is by far the most popular and has been the world standard for many years.

Much of the appeal of Excel is its versatility. Excel's forte, of course, is performing numerical calculations, but Excel is also useful for nonnumeric applications. Here are just a few uses for Excel:

Crunching numbers: Create budgets, tabulate expenses, analyze survey results, and perform just about any type of financial analysis you can think of.

Creating charts: Create a variety of highly customizable charts.

Organizing lists: Use the row-and-column layout to store lists efficiently.

Manipulating text: Clean up and standardize text-based data.

Accessing other data: Import data from a variety of sources such as databases, text files, web pages, and many others.

Creating graphical dashboards: Summarize a large amount of business information in a concise format.

Creating graphics and diagrams: Use shapes and illustrations to create professional-looking diagrams.

Automating complex tasks: Perform a tedious task with a single mouse click with Excel's macro capabilities.

Understanding Workbooks and Worksheets

An Excel file is called a *workbook*. You can have as many workbooks open as you need, and each one appears in its own window. By default, Excel workbooks use an `.xlsx` file extension.

> **NOTE**
>
> In old versions of Excel, every workbook opened in a single Excel window. Beginning with Excel 2013, each workbook opens in its own window. This change makes Excel work more like other Office applications and gives you the opportunity to put different workbooks on different monitors more easily.

The tabs in a workbook are called *worksheets*. Each workbook contains one or more worksheets, and each worksheet consists of individual cells. Each cell can contain a number, a formula, or text. A worksheet also has an invisible drawing layer, which holds charts, images, and diagrams. Objects on the drawing layer sit over the top of the cells, but they are not *in* the cells like a number or formula. You switch to a different worksheet by clicking its tab at the bottom of the workbook window. In addition, a workbook can store chart sheets; a chart sheet displays a single chart and is accessible by clicking a tab.

Don't be intimidated by all the different elements that appear within Excel's window. You don't need to know what all of them mean to use Excel effectively. And after you become familiar with the various parts, it all starts to make sense and you'll feel right at home.

Figure 1.1 shows you the more important bits and pieces of Excel. As you look at the figure, refer to Table 1.1 for a brief explanation of the items shown.

TABLE 1.1 Parts of the Excel screen that you need to know

Name	Description
Column letters	Letters range from A to XFD—one for each of the 16,384 columns in the worksheet. You can click a column heading to select an entire column or click between the column letters and drag to change the column width.
File button	Click this button to open Backstage view, which contains many options for working with your document (including printing) and setting Excel options.
Formula bar	When you enter information or formulas into a cell, it appears in this bar.
Horizontal scrollbar	Use this tool to scroll the sheet horizontally.
Macro recorder indicator	Click to start recording a Visual Basic for Applications (VBA) macro. The icon changes while your actions are being recorded. Click again to stop recording.
Name box	This box displays the active cell address or the name of the selected cell, range, or object.
New Sheet button	Add a new worksheet by clicking the New Sheet button (which is displayed after the last sheet tab).

Name	Description
Page view buttons	Click these buttons to change the way the worksheet is displayed.
Quick Access Toolbar	This customizable toolbar holds commonly used commands. The Quick Access Toolbar is always visible, regardless of which tab is selected.
Ribbon	This is the main location for Excel commands. Clicking an item in the tab list changes the Ribbon that is displayed.
Ribbon Display Options	A drop-down control that offers three options related to displaying the Ribbon.
Row numbers	Numbers range from 1 to 1,048,576—one for each row in the worksheet. You can click a row number to select an entire row or click between the row numbers and drag to change the row height.
Search box	Use this control to find commands or have Excel issue a command automatically. Alt+Q is the shortcut to access the Search box.
Selected cell indicator	This dark outline indicates the currently selected cell or range of cells. (There are 17,179,869,184 cells on each worksheet.)
Sheet tabs	Each of these notebook-like tabs represents a different sheet in the workbook. A workbook can have any number of sheets, and each sheet has its name displayed in a sheet tab.
Sheet tab controls	Use these buttons to scroll the sheet tabs to display tabs that aren't visible. You can also right-click to get a list of sheets.
Status bar	This bar displays various messages as well as summary information about the range of cells selected. Right-click the status bar to change which messages are displayed.
Tab list	Use these commands to display a different Ribbon.
Title bar	This displays the name of the program and the name of the current workbook. It also holds the Quick Access Toolbar (on the left), the Search box, and some control buttons that you can use to modify the window (on the right).
Vertical scrollbar	Use this tool to scroll the sheet vertically.
Window controls	There are three controls for minimizing the current window, maximizing or restoring the current window, and closing the current window, which are common to virtually all Windows applications.
Zoom control	Use this to zoom your worksheet in and out.

Moving Around a Worksheet

This section describes various ways to navigate the cells in a worksheet.

Every worksheet consists of rows (numbered 1 through 1,048,576) and columns (labeled A through XFD). Column labeling works like this: After column Z comes column AA, which is followed by AB, AC, and so on. After column AZ comes BA, BB, and so on. After column ZZ is AAA, AAB, and so on.

FIGURE 1.1

The Excel screen has many useful elements that you will use often.

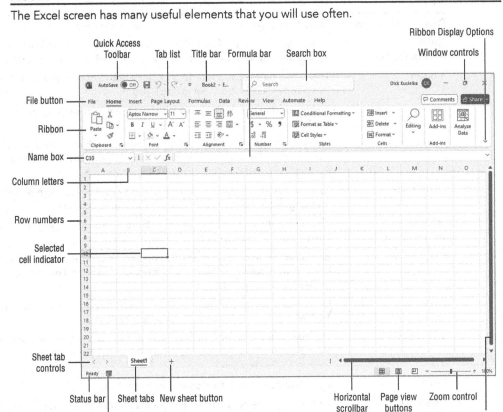

The intersection of a row and a column is a single cell, and each cell has a unique address made up of its column letter and row number. For example, the address of the upper-left cell is A1. The address of the cell at the lower right of a worksheet is XFD1048576.

At any given time, one cell is the active cell. The active cell is the cell that accepts keyboard input, and its contents can be edited. You can identify the active cell by its darker border, as shown in Figure 1.2. If more than one cell is selected, the dark border surrounds the entire selection, and the active cell is the light-colored cell within the border. Its address appears in the Name box. Depending on the technique you use to navigate through a workbook, you may or may not change the active cell when you navigate.

The row and column headings of the active cell appear in a different color to make it easier to identify the row and column of the active cell.

FIGURE 1.2

The active cell is the one with the dark border—in this case, cell C11.

	A	B	C	D
1		This Year	Last Year	
2	January	8,097	8,371	
3	February	7,985	7,567	
4	March	8,441	7,512	
5	April	8,088	7,453	
6	May	8,204	8,664	
7	June	7,114	7,466	
8	July	7,040	7,794	
9	August	7,265	7,018	
10	September	8,459	8,032	
11	October	8,982	8,637	
12	November	7,337	7,127	
13	December	7,799	7,331	
14				

NOTE

Excel is also available for devices that use a touch interface. This book assumes you have a traditional keyboard and mouse, so it doesn't cover the touch-related commands. Note that the drop-down control in the Quick Access Toolbar has a Touch/Mouse Mode command. In Touch mode, the Ribbon and Quick Access Toolbar icons are placed farther apart.

Navigating With Your Keyboard

Not surprisingly, you can use the standard navigational keys on your keyboard to move around a worksheet. These keys work just as you'd expect: The down arrow moves the active cell down one row, the right arrow moves it one column to the right, and so on. PgUp and PgDn move the active cell up or down one full window. (The actual number of rows moved depends on the number of rows displayed in the window.)

TIP

You can use the keyboard to scroll through the worksheet without changing the active cell by turning on Scroll Lock, which is useful if you need to view another area of your worksheet and then quickly return to your original location. Just press Scroll Lock and use the navigation keys to scroll through the worksheet. When you want to return to the original position (the active cell), press Ctrl+Backspace and then press Scroll Lock again to turn it off. When Scroll Lock is turned on, Excel displays `Scroll Lock` in the status bar at the bottom of the window.

The Num Lock key on your keyboard controls the way the keys on the numeric keypad behave. When Num Lock is on, the keys on your numeric keypad generate numbers. Many keyboards have a separate set of navigation (arrow) keys located to the left of the numeric keypad. The state of the Num Lock key doesn't affect these keys.

Table 1.2 summarizes all the worksheet movement keys available in Excel.

TABLE 1.2 **Excel worksheet movement keys**

Key	Action
Up arrow (↑) or Shift+Enter	Moves the active cell up one row
Down arrow (↓) or Enter	Moves the active cell down one row
Left arrow (←) or Shift+Tab	Moves the active cell one column to the left
Right arrow (→) or Tab	Moves the active cell one column to the right
PgUp	Moves the active cell up one screen
PgDn	Moves the active cell down one screen
Alt+PgDn	Moves the active cell right one screen
Alt+PgUp	Moves the active cell left one screen
Ctrl+Backspace	Scrolls the screen so that the active cell is visible
Ctrl+Home	Moves the active cell to A1
Ctrl+End	Moves the active cell to the bottom-rightmost cell on the worksheet's used range
↑*	Scrolls the screen up one row (active cell does not change)
↓*	Scrolls the screen down one row (active cell does not change)
←*	Scrolls the screen left one column (active cell does not change)
→*	Scrolls the screen right one column (active cell does not change)

* With Scroll Lock on

Navigating With Your Mouse

To change the active cell by using the mouse, just click another cell and it becomes the active cell. If the cell that you want to activate isn't visible in the workbook window, you can use the scrollbars to scroll the window in any direction. To scroll one cell, click either of the arrows on the scrollbar. To scroll by a complete screen, click either side of the scrollbar's scroll box. To scroll faster, drag the scroll box or right-click anywhere on the scrollbar for a menu of shortcuts.

TIP

If your mouse has a wheel, you can use it to scroll vertically. Also, if you click the wheel and move the mouse in any direction, the worksheet scrolls automatically in that direction. The more you move the mouse, the faster you scroll.

Press Ctrl while you use the mouse wheel to zoom the worksheet. If you prefer to use the mouse wheel to zoom the worksheet without pressing Ctrl, choose File ⇨ Options and select the Advanced section. Place a check mark next to the Zoom On Roll With IntelliMouse option.

Using the scrollbars or scrolling with your mouse doesn't change the active cell—it simply scrolls the worksheet. To change the active cell, you must click a new cell after scrolling.

Creating Your First Excel Workbook

IN THIS CHAPTER

■ Introducing Excel with a step-by-step hands-on session

This chapter presents an introductory, hands-on session with Excel. If you haven't used Excel, you may want to follow along on your computer to get a feel for how this software works.

In this example, you create a simple monthly sales projection table plus a chart that depicts the data.

Getting Started on Your Worksheet

Start Excel and make sure you have an empty workbook displayed. To create a new, blank workbook, press Ctrl+N (the shortcut key for File ➪ New ➪ Blank Workbook). Enter some sales projections in the new workbook.

The sales projections will consist of two columns of information. Column A will contain the month names, and column B will store the projected sales numbers. You start by entering some descriptive titles into the worksheet. Here's how to begin:

1. **Select cell A1 (the upper-left cell in the worksheet) by using the navigation (arrow) keys, if necessary.** The Name box displays the cell's address.

2. **Type Month into cell A1 and press Enter.** Depending on your setup, either Excel moves the selection to a different cell or the pointer remains in cell A1.

3. **Select cell B1, type Projected Sales, and press Enter.** The text extends beyond the cell width, but don't worry about that for now.

Filling In the Month Names

In this step, you enter the month names in column A.

1. **Select cell A2 and type Jan (an abbreviation for January).** At this point, you can enter the other month name abbreviations manually, or you can let Excel do some of the work by taking advantage of the AutoFill feature.

2. **Make sure that cell A2 is selected.** Notice that the active cell is displayed with a heavy outline. At the bottom-right corner of the outline, you'll see a small square known as the *fill handle*. Move your mouse pointer over the fill handle, click, and drag down until you've highlighted from cell A2 down to cell A13.

3. **Release the mouse button, and Excel automatically fills in the month names.**

Your worksheet should resemble the one shown in Figure 2.1.

FIGURE 2.1

Your worksheet after you've entered the column headings and month names

Entering the Sales Data

Next, you provide the sales projection numbers in column B. Assume that January's sales are projected to be $50,000 and that sales will increase by 3.5 percent in each subsequent month.

1. **Select cell B2 and type 50000, the projected sales for January.** You could type a dollar sign and comma to make the number more legible, but you'll do the number formatting a bit later.

2. **To enter a formula to calculate the projected sales for February, move to cell B3 and type the following:**

$$= B2 * 103.5\%$$

When you press Enter, the cell displays 51750. The formula returns the contents of cell B2, multiplied by 103.5 percent. In other words, February sales are projected to be 103.5 percent of the January sales—a 3.5 percent increase.

3. **The projected sales for subsequent months use a similar formula, but rather than retype the formula for each cell in column B, take advantage of the AutoFill**

feature. Make sure that cell B3 is selected. Click the cell's fill handle, drag down to cell B13, and release the mouse button.

At this point, your worksheet should resemble the one shown in Figure 2.2. Keep in mind that, except for cell B2, the values in column B are calculated with formulas. To demonstrate, try changing the projected sales value for the initial month, January (in cell B2). You'll find that the formulas recalculate and return different values. All these formulas depend on the initial value in cell B2.

FIGURE 2.2

Your worksheet after you've created the formulas

	A	B	C
1	Month	Projected Sales	
2	Jan	50000	
3	Feb	51750	
4	Mar	53561.25	
5	Apr	55435.89	
6	May	57376.15	
7	Jun	59384.32	
8	Jul	61462.77	
9	Aug	63613.96	
10	Sep	65840.45	
11	Oct	68144.87	
12	Nov	70529.94	
13	Dec	72998.49	
14			
15			

Formatting the Numbers

The values in the worksheet are difficult to read because they aren't formatted. In this step, you apply a number format to make the numbers easier to read and more consistent in appearance.

1. **Select the numbers by clicking cell B2 and dragging down to cell B13.** Don't drag the fill handle this time, though, because you're selecting cells, not filling a range.

2. **Access the Ribbon and click Home.** In the Number group, click the drop-down Number Format control (it initially displays General), and select Currency from the

list. The numbers now display with a currency symbol and two decimal places. That's much better, but the decimal places aren't necessary for this type of projection.

3. **Make sure that the range B2:B13 is selected, choose Home ⇨ Number, and click the Decrease Decimal button.** One of the decimal places disappears. Click that button a second time and the values are displayed with no decimal places.

Making Your Worksheet Look a Bit Fancier

At this point, you have a functional worksheet, but it could use some help in the appearance department. Converting this range to an "official" (and attractive) Excel table is a snap.

1. **Activate any cell within the range A1:B13.**

2. **Choose Insert ⇨ Tables ⇨ Table.** Excel displays the Create Table dialog box to make sure that it guessed the range properly.

3. **Click OK to close the Create Table dialog box.** Excel applies its default table formatting and displays its Table Design contextual tab.

Your worksheet should look like Figure 2.3.

FIGURE 2.3

Your worksheet after you've converted the range to a table

Month	Projected Sales
Jan	$50,000
Feb	$51,750
Mar	$53,561
Apr	$55,436
May	$57,376
Jun	$59,384
Jul	$61,463
Aug	$63,614
Sep	$65,840
Oct	$68,145
Nov	$70,530
Dec	$72,998

If you don't like the default table style, just select another one from the Table Design ⇨ Table Styles group. Notice that you can get a preview of different table styles by moving your mouse over the Ribbon. When you find one you like, click it, and the style will be applied to your table.

 See Chapter 8, "Working with Tables," for more information on Excel tables.

Summing the Values

The worksheet displays the monthly projected sales, but what about the total projected sales for the year? Because this range is a table, it's simple.

1. **Activate any cell in the table.**
2. **Choose Table Design ⇨ Table Style Options ⇨ Total Row.** Excel automatically adds a new row to the bottom of your table, including a formula that calculates the total of the Projected Sales column.
3. **If you'd prefer to see a different summary formula (e.g., average), click cell B14 and choose a different summary formula from the drop-down list.**

Creating a Chart

How about a chart that shows the projected sales for each month?

1. **Activate any cell in the table.**
2. **Choose Insert ⇨ Charts ⇨ Recommended Charts.** Excel displays some suggested chart type options.
3. **In the Insert Chart dialog box, click the second recommended chart (a column chart), and click OK.** Excel inserts the chart in the center of the window. To move the chart to another location, click its border and drag it.
4. **Click the chart and choose a style using the Chart Design ⇨ Chart Styles options.**

Figure 2.4 shows the worksheet with a column chart. Your chart may look different, depending on the chart style you selected.

FIGURE 2.4

The table and chart

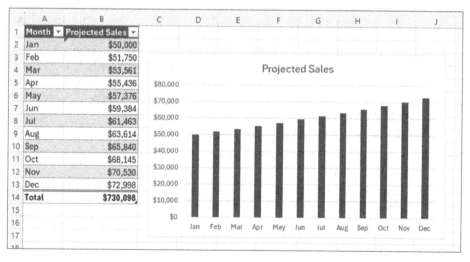

This workbook is available on this book's website at www.wiley.com/go/excelquickandeasy. The filename is `table and chart.xlsx`.

Printing Your Worksheet

Printing your worksheet is easy (assuming that you have a printer attached and that it works properly).

1. **Make sure that the chart isn't selected.** If a chart is selected, the chart will print on a page by itself. To deselect the chart, just press Esc or click any cell.

2. **To make use of Excel's handy Page Layout view, click the Page Layout button on the right side of the status bar.** Excel displays the worksheet page by page so that you can easily see how your printed output will look. In Page Layout view, you can tell immediately whether the chart is too wide to fit on one page. If the chart is too wide, click and drag a corner of the chart to resize it or just move the chart below the table of numbers. Click the Normal button to return to the default view.

3. **When you're ready to print, choose File ⇨ Print.** At this point, you can change some print settings. For example, you can choose to print in landscape rather than portrait orientation. Make the change, and you see the result in the preview window.

4. **When you're satisfied, click the large Print button in the upper-left corner.** The page is printed, and you're returned to your workbook.

Saving Your Workbook

Until now, everything that you've done has occurred in your computer's memory. If the power should fail, all may be lost—unless Excel's AutoRecover feature happened to kick in. It's time to save your work to a file on your hard drive.

1. **Click the Save button on the Quick Access Toolbar.** (This button looks like an old-fashioned floppy disk, popular in the previous century.) Because the workbook hasn't been saved yet and still has its default name, Excel responds with a Save This File dialog box that lets you choose the location for the workbook file. The Choose A Location drop-down lists some recently used locations, or you can click More Options to see the Save As Backstage screen. From there, you can click Browse to navigate to any location on your computer.

2. **Click Browse.** Excel displays the Save As dialog box.

3. **In the File Name field, enter a name (such as Monthly Sales Projection).** If you like, you can specify a different location.

4. **Click Save or press Enter.** Excel saves the workbook as a file. The workbook remains open so that you can work with it some more.

NOTE

By default, Excel saves a backup copy of your work automatically every 10 minutes. To adjust the AutoRecover setting (or turn it off), choose File ⟶ Options and click the Save tab of the Excel Options dialog box. However, you should never rely on Excel's AutoRecover feature. Saving your work frequently is a good idea.

If you've followed along, you probably have realized that creating this workbook was not difficult. But, of course, you've barely scratched the surface of Excel. The remainder of this book covers these tasks (and many, many more) in much greater detail.

TIP

Excel's Backstage view has a section for pinned folders at the top of the list of recent folders. If you use a particular folder often, you can pin it to the top of the list to make it more accessible. To pin a folder, find it in the list of recent folders, hover your mouse pointer over the folder, and click the push pin icon.

2

Entering and Editing Worksheet Data

IN THIS CHAPTER

- Understanding the types of data you can use
- Entering text and values into your worksheets
- Entering dates and times into your worksheets
- Modifying and editing information

This chapter describes what you need to know about entering and modifying data in your worksheets. As you'll see, Excel doesn't treat all data equally. Therefore, you need to learn about the various types of data you can use in an Excel worksheet.

Exploring Data Types

An Excel workbook file can hold any number of worksheets, and each worksheet is made up of more than 17 billion cells. A cell can hold any of four basic types of data:

- A numeric value
- Text
- A formula
- An error

A worksheet can also hold charts, diagrams, buttons, and other objects. These objects aren't contained in cells. Instead, they reside on the worksheet's drawing layer, which is an invisible layer on top of each worksheet. Pictures can reside either on the drawing layer or, in more recent versions of Excel, directly in a cell.

 Chapter 5, "Moving Beyond Formula Basics," discusses how to correct common formula errors.

Numeric Values

Numeric values represent a quantity of some type: sales amounts, number of employees, atomic weights, test scores, and so on. Values also can be dates (such as Feb 26, 2022) or times (such as 3:24 AM).

Excel's Numeric Limitations

You may be curious about the types of values Excel can handle. In other words, how large can a number be? How accurate are large numbers?

Excel's numbers are precise up to 15 digits. For example, if you enter a large value, such as 123,456,789,123,456,789 (18 digits), Excel actually stores it with only 15 digits of precision. This 18-digit number displays as 123,456,789,123,456,000. This precision may seem quite limiting, but in practice, it rarely causes any problems.

One situation in which the 15-digit precision can cause a problem is when entering credit card numbers. Most credit card numbers are 16 digits, but Excel can handle only 15 digits, so it substitutes a zero for the last credit card digit. Even worse, you may not even realize that Excel made the card number invalid. The solution? Enter the credit card numbers as text. The easiest way is to preformat the cell as Text. (Choose Home ➪ Number, and choose Text from the Number Format drop-down list.) Or you can precede the credit card number with an apostrophe. Either method prevents Excel from interpreting the entry as a number.

Here are some of Excel's other numeric limits:

- Largest positive number: 9.9E+307
- Smallest negative number: –9.9E+307
- Smallest positive number: 2.2251E–308
- Largest negative number: –2.2251E–308

These numbers are expressed in scientific notation. For example, the largest positive number is "9.9 times 10 to the 307th power"—in other words, 99 followed by 306 zeros. Keep in mind, though, that this number has only 15 digits of precision.

Text Entries

Most worksheets also include text in some of the cells. Text can serve as data (e.g., a list of employee names), labels for values, headings for columns, or instructions about the worksheet. Text is often used to clarify what the values in a worksheet mean or where the numbers came from.

Text that begins with a number is still considered text. For example, if you type **12 Employees** into a cell, Excel considers the entry to be text rather than a numeric value. Consequently, you can't use this cell for numeric calculations. If you need to indicate that the number 12 refers to employees, enter **12** into a cell and then type **Employees** into an adjacent cell.

Formulas

Formulas are what make a spreadsheet a spreadsheet. Excel enables you to enter flexible formulas that use the values (or even text) in cells to calculate a result. When you enter a formula into a cell, the formula's result appears in the cell. If you change any of the cells used by a formula, the formula recalculates and shows the new result.

Formulas can be simple mathematical expressions, or they can use some of the powerful functions that are built into Excel. Figure 3.1 shows an Excel worksheet set up to calculate a monthly loan payment. The worksheet contains values, text, and formulas. The cells in column A contain text. Column B contains four values and two formulas. The formulas are in cells B6 and B10. Column D, for reference, shows the actual contents of the cells in column B.

FIGURE 3.1

You can use values, text, and formulas to create useful Excel worksheets.

	A	B	C	D	E
1	**Loan Payment Calculator**				
2					
3				Column B Contents	
4	Purchase Amount:	$475,000		475000	
5	Down Payment Pct:	20%		0.2	
6	Loan Amount:	$380,000		=B4*(1-B5)	
7	Term (months):	360		360	
8	Interest Rate (APR):	7.48%		0.0748	
9					
10	**Monthly Payment:**	$2,651.81		=PMT(B8/12,B7,-B6)	
11					

 This workbook, named `loan payment calculator.xlsx`, is available on this book's website at www.wiley.com/go/excelquickandeasy.

 You can find out much more about formulas in Chapters 4 and 5.

Error Values

The fourth data type cells can hold is an error value. Error values are the results of formulas that contain an error, like the #VALUE! error that results from trying to do addition on a text entry. When a formula returns an error, any formulas that use that result will show the same error.

Entering Text and Values into Your Worksheets

If you've ever worked in a desktop application, like on Windows or macOS, you'll find that entering data into worksheet cells is simple and intuitive. And while there are differences in how Excel stores and displays the different data types, for the most part it just works.

Entering Numbers

To enter a numeric value into a cell, select the appropriate cell, type the value, and then press Enter, Tab, or one of the arrow navigation keys. The value is displayed in the cell and appears in the Formula bar when the cell is selected. You can include decimal points and currency symbols when entering values, along with plus signs, minus signs, percent signs, and commas (to separate thousands). If you precede a value with a minus sign or enclose it in parentheses, Excel considers it to be a negative number.

Entering Text

Entering text into a cell is just as easy as entering a value: Activate the cell, type the text, and then press Enter or a navigation key. A cell can contain a maximum of about 32,000 characters—more than enough to store a typical chapter in this book. Even though a cell can hold a huge number of characters, you'll find that it's not actually possible to display all of these characters.

TIP

If you type an exceptionally long text entry into a cell, the Formula bar may not show all the text. To display more of the text in the Formula bar, click the bottom of the Formula bar and drag down to increase the height (see Figure 3.2). Also useful is the Ctrl+Shift+U keyboard shortcut. Pressing this key combination toggles the height of the Formula bar to show either one row or the previous size.

FIGURE 3.2

The Formula bar, expanded in height to show more information in the cell

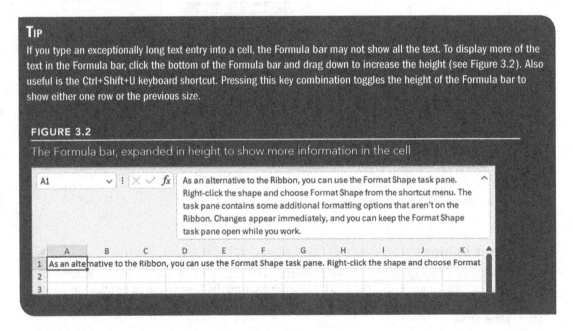

What happens when you enter text that's longer than its column's current width? If the cells to the immediate right are blank, Excel displays the text in its entirety, appearing to spill the entry into adjacent cells. If an adjacent cell isn't blank, Excel displays as much of the text as possible. (The full text is contained in the cell; it's just not displayed.) If you need to display a long text string in a cell that's adjacent to a nonblank cell, you have a few choices:

- Edit your text to make it shorter.
- Increase the width of the column (drag the border between column letters in the header).
- Use a smaller font.
- Wrap the text within the cell so that it occupies more than one line. Choose Home ➪ Alignment ➪ Wrap Text to toggle wrapping on and off for the selected cell or range.

Using Enter Mode

The left side of Excel's status bar normally displays "Ready," indicating that Excel is ready for you to enter or edit data in the worksheet. If you start typing numbers or text in a cell, the status bar changes to display "Enter" to indicate you're in *Enter mode*. The most common modes for Excel to be in are Ready, Enter, and Edit. See "Modifying Cell Contents" later in this chapter for more information about Edit mode.

In Enter mode, you are actively entering something into a cell. As you type, the text shows in the cell and in the Formula bar. You haven't actually changed the contents of the cell until you leave Enter mode, which commits the value to the cell. To leave Enter mode, you can press Enter, Tab, or just about any navigation key on your keyboard (like PgUp or Home). The value you typed is committed to the cell, and the status bar changes back to say "Ready."

You can also leave Enter mode by pressing the Esc key. Pressing Esc ignores your changes and returns the cell to its previous value.

Entering Dates and Times into Your Worksheets

Excel treats dates and times as special types of numeric values. Dates and times are values that are formatted so that they appear as dates or times. If you work with dates and times, you need to understand Excel's date and time system.

Entering Date Values

Excel handles dates by using a serial number system. The earliest date that Excel understands is January 1, 1900. This date has a serial number of 1; January 2, 1900, has a serial number of 2; and so on. This system makes it easy to deal with dates in formulas. For example, you can enter a formula to calculate the number of days between two dates.

Most of the time, you don't have to be concerned with Excel's serial number date system. You can simply enter a date in a common date format, and Excel takes care of the details behind the scenes. For example, if you need to enter June 1, 2024, you can enter the date by typing **June 1, 2024** (or use any of several different date formats). Excel interprets your entry and stores the value 45444, which is the serial number for that date.

> **NOTE**
>
> The date examples in this book use the U.S. English system. Your Windows regional settings will affect the way Excel interprets a date that you've entered. For example, depending on your regional date settings, June 1, 2024, may be interpreted as text rather than as a date. In such a case, you need to enter the date in a format that corresponds to your regional date settings—for example, 1 June 2024.

Entering Time Values

When you work with times, you extend Excel's date serial number system to include decimals. In other words, Excel works with times by using fractional days. For example, the date serial number for June 1, 2024, is 45444. Noon on June 1, 2024 (halfway through the day), is represented internally as 45444.5 because the time fraction is added to the date serial number to get the full date/time serial number.

Again, you normally don't have to be concerned with these serial numbers or fractional serial numbers for times. Just enter the time into a cell in a recognized format. In this case, type **June 1, 2024 12:00**.

Modifying Cell Contents

After you enter a value or text into a cell, you can modify it in several ways:

- Delete the cell's contents.
- Replace the cell's contents with something else.
- Edit the cell's contents.

> **NOTE**
> You can also modify a cell by changing its formatting. However, formatting a cell affects only a cell's appearance. Formatting doesn't affect the cell's contents. See Chapter 9, "Formatting Worksheets," to learn more.

Deleting the Contents of a Cell

To delete the contents of a cell, just click the cell and press the Delete key. To delete the contents of more than one cell, select all the cells that you want to delete and then press Delete. Pressing Delete removes the cell's contents but doesn't remove any formatting (such as bold, italic, or the number format) that you may have applied to the cell.

For more control over what gets deleted, you can choose Home ⇨ Editing ⇨ Clear. This command's drop-down list has six choices.

- **Clear All:** Clears everything from the cell—its contents, formatting, and cell comment (if it has one).
- **Clear Formats:** Clears only the formatting and leaves the value, text, or formula.
- **Clear Contents:** Clears only the cell's value, text, or formula and leaves the formatting. This has the same effect as pressing Delete.
- **Clear Comments And Notes:** Clears the comment or note (if one exists) attached to the cell.
- **Clear Hyperlinks:** Removes hyperlinks contained in the selected cells. The text and formatting remain, so the cell still looks like it has a hyperlink, but it no longer functions as a hyperlink.
- **Remove Hyperlinks:** Removes hyperlinks in the selected cells, including the cell formatting.

> **NOTE**
>
> Clearing formats doesn't clear the background colors in a range that has been designated as a table except in two circumstances: If you select the entire table or you've replaced the table style background colors manually, the table formatting will be cleared. See Chapter 8, "Working with Tables," for more about tables.

Replacing the Contents of a Cell

To replace the contents of a cell with something else, just activate the cell, type your new entry, and press Enter or a navigation key. Any formatting applied to the cell remains in place and is applied to the new content.

You can also replace cell contents by dragging and dropping or by copying and pasting data from another cell. In both cases, the cell formatting will be replaced by the format of the new data. To avoid pasting formatting, choose Home ⇨ Clipboard ⇨ Paste ⇨ Values (V), or Home ⇨ Clipboard ⇨ Paste ⇨ Formulas (F).

Editing the Contents of a Cell

If the cell contains only a few characters, replacing its contents by typing new data usually is easiest. However, if the cell contains lengthy text or a complex formula and you need to make only a slight modification, you probably want to edit the cell rather than reenter information.

When you want to edit the contents of a cell, you can use one of the following ways to enter Edit mode:

- Double-click the cell to edit the cell contents directly in the cell.
- Select the cell and press F2 to edit the cell contents directly in the cell.
- Select the cell that you want to edit and then click inside the Formula bar to edit the cell contents in the Formula bar.

You can use whichever method you prefer. Some people find editing directly in the cell easier; others prefer to use the Formula bar to edit a cell.

> **NOTE**
>
> The Advanced tab of the Excel Options dialog box contains a section called Editing Options. These settings affect how editing works. (To access this dialog box, choose File ⇨ Options.) If the Allow Editing Directly In Cells option isn't enabled, you can't edit a cell by double-clicking. In addition, pressing F2 allows you to edit the cell in the Formula bar (not directly in the cell).

All these methods cause Excel to go into Edit mode. (The word *Edit* appears at the left side of the status bar at the bottom of the window.) When Excel is in Edit mode, the Formula bar enables two icons: Cancel (the X) and Enter (the check mark). Figure 3.3 shows these two icons. Clicking the Cancel icon cancels editing without changing the cell's contents. (Pressing

3

Esc has the same effect.) Clicking the Enter icon completes the editing and enters the modified contents into the cell. (Pressing Enter has the same effect, except that clicking the Enter icon doesn't change the active cell.)

FIGURE 3.3

When you're editing a cell, the Formula bar enables two new icons: Cancel (X) and Enter (check mark).

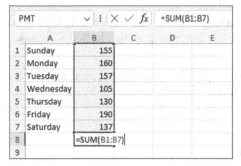

When you begin editing a cell, the insertion point appears as a vertical bar, and you can perform the following tasks:

- Add new characters at the location of the insertion point.
- Move the insertion point by doing one of the following:
  - Using the navigation keys to move within the cell
  - Pressing Home to move the insertion point to the beginning of the cell
  - Pressing End to move the insertion point to the end of the cell
- Select multiple characters. Press Shift while you use the navigation keys.
- Select characters while you're editing a cell. Use the mouse. Just click and drag the mouse pointer over the characters that you want to select.
- Delete a character to the left of the insertion point. The Backspace key deletes one character to the left of the insertion point. It has no effect if the insertion point is at the start of the text.
- Delete a character to the right of the insertion point. The Delete key deletes one character to the right of the insertion point. It has no effect if the insertion point is at the end of the text.

NOTE

If you are editing a cell and have multiple characters selected, the Backspace and Delete keys work the same. Either deletes the selected text, regardless of whether it is to the left or right of the insertion point.

Learning Some Handy Data-Entry Techniques

You can simplify the process of entering information into your Excel worksheets and make your work go quite a bit faster by using a number of useful tricks, which are described in the following sections.

Automatically Moving the Selection After Entering Data

By default, Excel automatically selects the next cell down when you press the Enter key after entering data into a cell. To change this setting, choose File ⇨ Options and click the Advanced tab (see Figure 3.4). The check box that controls this behavior is labeled After Pressing Enter, Move Selection. If you enable this option, you can choose the direction in which the selection moves (down, right, up, or left).

FIGURE 3.4

You can use the Advanced tab in the Excel Options dialog box to select several helpful input option settings.

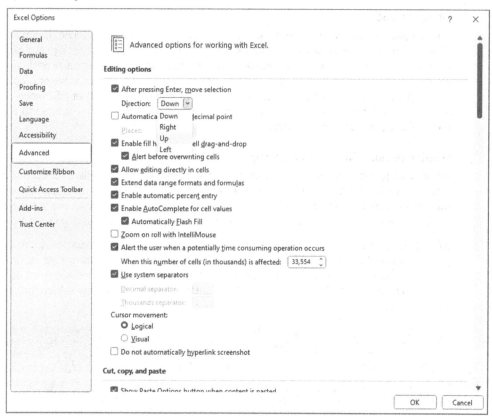

Selecting a Range of Input Cells Before Entering Data

When a range of cells is selected, Excel automatically selects the next cell in the range when you press Enter, even if you disabled the After Pressing Enter, Move Selection option. If the selection consists of multiple rows, Excel moves down the column; when it reaches the end of the selection in the column, it moves to the first selected cell in the next column.

To skip a cell, just press Enter without entering anything. To go backward, press Shift+Enter. If you prefer to enter the data by rows rather than by columns, press Tab rather than Enter. Excel continues to cycle through the selected range until you select a cell outside the range. Any of the navigation keys, like the arrow keys or the Home key, will change the selected range. If you want to navigate within the selected range, you must stick to Enter and Tab.

Using Ctrl+Enter to Place Information into Multiple Cells Simultaneously

If you need to enter the same data into multiple cells, Excel offers a handy shortcut. Select all the cells that you want to contain the data; enter the value, text, or formula; and then press Ctrl+Enter. The same information is inserted into each cell in the selection.

Changing Modes

You can press F2 to change between Enter mode and Edit mode. For example, if you're typing a long sentence in Enter mode and you realize that you spelled a word wrong, you can press F2 to change to Edit mode. In Edit mode, you can move through the sentence with your arrow keys to fix the misspelled word. You can also use the Ctrl+arrow keys to move one word at a time instead of one character at a time. You can continue to enter text in Edit mode or return to Enter mode by pressing F2 again, after which the navigation keys can be used to commit the text and move to a different cell.

Entering Decimal Points Automatically

If you need to enter lots of numbers with a fixed number of decimal places, Excel has a useful tool that works like some old adding machines. Access the Excel Options dialog box and click the Advanced tab. Select the Automatically Insert A Decimal Point option and make sure that the Places box is set for the correct number of decimal places for the data you need to enter.

When this option is set, Excel supplies the decimal points for you automatically. For example, if you specify two decimal places, entering **12345** into a cell is interpreted as 123.45. To restore things to normal, just deselect the Automatically Insert A Decimal Point option in the Excel Options dialog box. Changing this setting doesn't affect any values that you already entered.

CAUTION

The fixed decimal places option is a global setting and applies to all workbooks (not just the active workbook). If you forget that this option is turned on, you can easily end up entering incorrect values—or cause some major confusion if someone else uses your computer.

Using AutoFill to Enter a Series of Values

The Excel AutoFill feature makes inserting a series of values or text items in a range of cells easy. It uses the *fill handle* (the small box at the lower right of the active cell or range). You can drag the fill handle to copy the cell or automatically complete a series.

Figure 3.5 shows an example. Enter **1** into cell A1, and enter **3** into cell A2. Then select both cells and drag down the fill handle to create a linear series of odd numbers. The figure also shows an icon that, when clicked, displays some additional AutoFill options. This icon appears only if the Show Paste Options Button When Content Is Pasted option is selected in the Advanced tab of the Excel Options dialog box.

FIGURE 3.5

This series was created by using AutoFill.

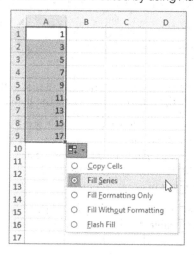

Excel uses the cells' data to guess the pattern. If you start with 1 and 2, it will guess you want each cell to go up by 1. If, as in the previous example, you start with 1 and 3, it guesses that you want the increment to be 2. Excel does a good job of guessing date patterns, too. If you start with 1/31/2024 and 2/29/2024, it will fill the last day of the successive months.

> **TIP**
>
> If you drag the fill handle while you press and hold the right mouse button, Excel displays a shortcut menu with additional fill options. You can also use Home ➪ Editing ➪ Fill for even more control over automatically filling a range.

Using AutoComplete to Automate Data Entry

The Excel AutoComplete feature makes entering the same text into multiple cells easy. With AutoComplete, you type the first few letters of a text entry into a cell, and Excel automatically completes the entry based on other entries that you already made in the column. Besides reducing typing, this feature ensures that your entries are spelled correctly and are consistent.

Here's how it works: Suppose you're entering product information into a column. One of your products is named Widgets. The first time you enter **Widgets** into a cell, Excel remembers it. Later, when you start typing **Widgets** in that same column, Excel recognizes it by the first few letters and finishes typing it for you. Just press Enter, and you're done. To override the suggestion, just keep typing.

AutoComplete also changes the case of letters for you automatically. If you start entering **widgets** (with a lowercase *w*) in the second entry, Excel makes the *w* uppercase to be consistent with the previous entry in the column.

> **TIP**
>
> You also can access a mouse-oriented version of AutoComplete by right-clicking the cell and choosing Pick From Drop-down List from the shortcut menu. Excel then displays a drop-down box that has all of the text entries in the current column, and you just click the one that you want.

Keep in mind that AutoComplete works only within a contiguous column of cells. If you have a blank row, for example, AutoComplete identifies only the cell contents below the blank row.

Sometimes, Excel will use AutoComplete to try to finish a word when you don't want it to do so. If you type **canister** in a cell and then below it type the shorter word **can**, Excel will attempt to AutoComplete the entry to *canister*. When you want to type a word that starts with the same letters as an AutoComplete entry but is shorter, simply press the Delete key when you've reached the end of the word and then press Enter or a navigation key.

If you find the AutoComplete feature distracting, you can turn it off by using the Advanced tab of the Excel Options dialog box. Simply deselect Enable AutoComplete For Cell Values.

Forcing Text to Appear on a New Line Within a Cell

If you have lengthy text in a cell, you can force Excel to display it in multiple lines within the cell; press Alt+Enter to start a new line in a cell.

When you add a line break, Excel automatically changes the cell's format to Wrap Text. But unlike normal text wrap, your manual line break forces Excel to break the text at a specific place within the text, which gives you more precise control over the appearance of the text than if you rely on automatic text wrapping.

> **TIP**
>
> To remove a manual line break, edit the cell and press Delete when the insertion point is located at the end of the line that contains the manual line break. You won't see any symbol to indicate the position of the manual line break, but the text that follows it will move up when the line break is deleted.

Using AutoCorrect for Shorthand Data Entry

You can use the AutoCorrect feature to create shortcuts for commonly used words or phrases. For example, if you work for a company named Consolidated Data Processing Corporation, you can create an AutoCorrect entry for an abbreviation, such as *cdp*. Then, whenever you type **cdp** and take an action to trigger AutoCorrect (such as typing a space, pressing Enter, or selecting a different cell), Excel automatically changes the text to Consolidated Data Processing Corporation.

Excel includes quite a few built-in AutoCorrect terms (mostly to correct common misspellings), and you can add your own. To set up your custom AutoCorrect entries, access the Excel Options dialog box (choose File ⇨ Options) and click the Proofing tab. Then click the AutoCorrect Options button to display the AutoCorrect dialog box. In the dialog box, click the AutoCorrect tab, select Replace Text As You Type, and then enter your custom entries. (Figure 3.6 shows an example.) You can set up as many custom entries as you like. Just be careful not to use an abbreviation that might appear normally in your text.

FIGURE 3.6

AutoCorrect allows you to create shorthand abbreviations for text you enter often.

3

> **TIP**
>
> Excel shares your AutoCorrect list with other Microsoft Office applications. For example, any AutoCorrect entries you created in Word also work in Excel.

Entering Numbers with Fractions

Most of the time, you'll want non-integer values to be displayed with decimal points. But Excel can also display values with fractions. To enter a fractional value into a cell, leave a space between the whole number and the fraction. For example, to enter 6 7/8, enter **6 7/8** and then press Enter. When you select the cell, 6.875 appears in the Formula bar, and the cell entry appears as a fraction. If you have a fraction only (e.g., 1/8), you must enter a zero first, like this—**0 1/8**—or Excel will likely assume that you're entering a date. When you select the cell and look at the Formula bar, you see 0.125. In the cell, you see 1/8.

Using a Form for Data Entry

Many people use Excel to manage lists in which the information is arranged in rows. Excel offers a simple way to work with this type of data using a data entry form that Excel can create automatically. This data form works with either a normal range of data or a range that has been designated as a table. (Choose Insert ➪ Tables ➪ Table.) Figure 3.7 shows an example.

FIGURE 3.7

Excel's built-in data form can simplify many data-entry tasks.

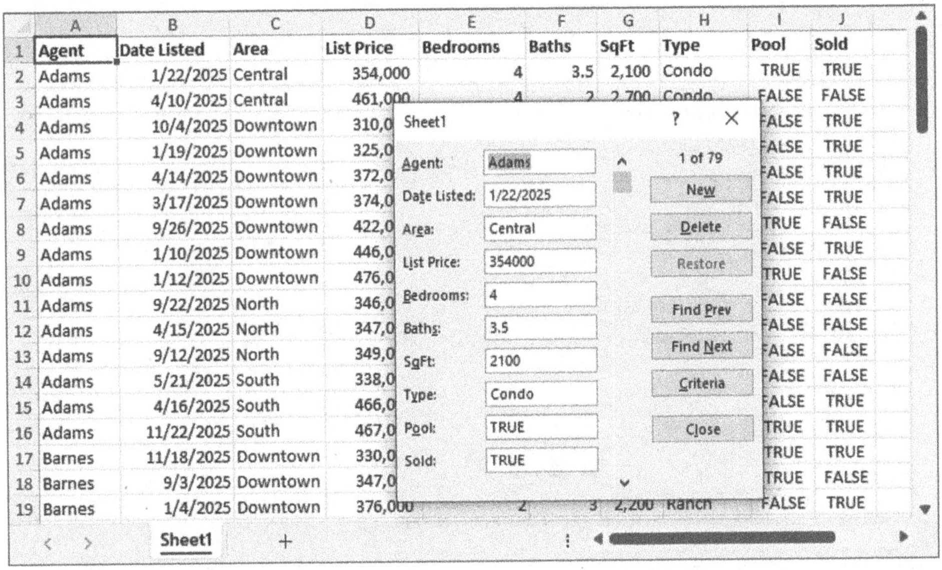

Unfortunately, the command to access the data form is not on the Ribbon. To use the data form, you must add it to your Quick Access Toolbar, add it to the Ribbon, or search for Form in the Search box. Here's how to add this command to your Quick Access Toolbar:

1. Right-click the Quick Access Toolbar and choose Customize Quick Access Toolbar. The Quick Access Toolbar panel of the Excel Options dialog box appears.

2. In the Choose Commands From drop-down list, choose Commands Not In The Ribbon.

3. In the list box on the left, select Form.

4. Click the Add button to add the selected command to your Quick Access Toolbar.

5. Click OK to close the Excel Options dialog box.

After you perform these steps, a new icon appears on your Quick Access Toolbar.

To use a data entry form, follow these steps:

1. Arrange your data so that Excel can recognize it as a table by entering headings for the columns into the first row of your data entry range.

2. Select any cell in the table and click the Form button on your Quick Access Toolbar. Excel displays a dialog box customized to your data (refer to the example in Figure 3.7).

3. Fill in the information. Press Tab to move between the text boxes. If a cell contains a formula, the formula result appears as text (not as an edit box). In other words, you can't modify formulas using the data entry form.

4. When you complete the data form, click the New button. Excel enters the data into a row in the worksheet and clears the dialog box for the next row of data.

You can also use the form to edit existing data.

 This workbook is available on this book's website at www.wiley.com/go/excelquickandeasy. **The file is named** data form.xlsx.

Entering the Current Date or Time into a Cell

If you need to date-stamp or time-stamp your worksheet, Excel provides two shortcut keys that do this task for you:

- **Current date:** Ctrl+; (semicolon)
- **Current time:** Ctrl+Shift+; (semicolon)

To enter both the date and time, press Ctrl+;, type a space, and then press Ctrl+Shift+;.

The date and time are from the system time in your computer. If the date or time isn't correct in Excel, use the Windows Settings to make the adjustment.

NOTE

When you use the Ctrl+; or the Ctrl+Shift+; shortcut to enter a date or time into your worksheet, Excel enters a static value into the worksheet. In other words, the date or time entered doesn't change when the worksheet is recalculated. In most cases, this setup is probably what you want, but you should be aware of this limitation. If you want the date or time display to update, use one of these functions:

```
=TODAY()
=NOW()
```

3

Introducing Formulas and Functions

IN THIS CHAPTER

- Understanding formula basics
- Entering formulas and functions into your worksheets
- Understanding how to use cell references in formulas

xcel is, at its core, a calculation engine. Like a calculator, Excel accepts questions in the form of a formula (such as =2+2) and returns an answer. Formulas allow you to perform not only mathematical operations, but also a myriad of other complex actions. With formulas, you can parse textual values, look up data based on specific criteria, and perform conditional analysis. If it weren't for formulas, a spreadsheet would simply be a fancy word processing document that has great support for tabular information.

If you want to leverage the full power of Excel, it's important to understand how formulas work. This chapter introduces formulas and functions and helps you to get up to speed with writing your own formulas.

Understanding Formula Basics

Each cell in a worksheet is given a name based on its position. The top-leftmost cell is called A1. It's located in column A, row 1. When you enter a value in cell A1 (for example, the number 5), that cell's value becomes 5. Entering the number 10 in cell B1 will make that cell's value 10. You can then use these values in a formula.

For instance, you can click in cell C1 and begin typing =A1+B1. After you press the Enter key, Excel recognizes what you're asking and performs the calculation that gives you the result of 15 (5 + 10 = 15).

A formula always begins with an equal sign and can contain any of these elements:

- **Constants:** Hard-coded numbers can be used directly in a formula. For example, you can enter =5+10 directly into a cell to get the answer 15.
- **Operators:** These include symbols that designate mathematical operations such as + (for addition) and * (for multiplication). Some operators compare values (>, <, =), while others

join values together (&). As you may have guessed, you can mix constants and operators to create a formula. For instance, entering =15>10 into a cell would return TRUE as the result because 15 is indeed greater than 10.

- **Cell references:** These include any value that points back to a single cell or a range of cells. When you enter =A1+B1 into a cell, you are essentially using two cell references. Cell references tell Excel to use the values in the cells being referenced in the formula.
- **Text strings:** Any text string can be used as an argument in a formula as long as it's wrapped in quotes. For instance, entering ="Microsoft"&" "&"Excel" into any cell will result in the joined text "Microsoft Excel."
- **Worksheet functions:** You can use a virtually unlimited combination of Excel functions (such as SUM and AVERAGE) to build your formulas. For example, clicking on cell B1 and entering =SUM(A1:A10) will add all the values in cells A1 through A10.

After you enter a formula, the cell containing your formula displays the calculated result. While your formula cell displays the result, the Formula bar will always show the formula.

Table 4.1 lists a few examples of formulas.

TABLE 4.1 Example formulas and their results

Example formula	Result
=150*.05	Multiplies 150 by 0.05. This formula uses only values, and it always returns the same result. You could just enter the value 7.5 into the cell, but using a formula provides information on how the value was calculated.
=A3	Displays the value from cell A3. No calculation is performed on A3.
=A1+A2	Adds the values in cells A1 and A2.
=Income-Expenses	Subtracts the value in the cell named Expenses from the value in the cell named Income.
=SUM(A1:A12)	Adds the values in the range A1:A12, using the SUM function.
=A1=C12	Compares cell A1 with cell C12. If the cells are the same, the formula returns TRUE; otherwise, it returns FALSE.

Again, note that every formula begins with an equal sign (=). The initial equals sign allows Excel to distinguish a formula from plain text.

Using Operators in Formulas

Excel formulas support a variety of operators. Operators are symbols that indicate what mathematical (or logical) operation you want the formula to perform. Table 4.2 lists the operators that Excel recognizes. In addition to these, Excel has many built-in functions that enable you to perform additional calculations.

TABLE 4.2 Operators used in formulas

Operator	Name
+	Addition
–	Subtraction
*	Multiplication
/	Division
^	Exponentiation
&	Concatenation
=	Logical comparison (equal to)
>	Logical comparison (greater than)
<	Logical comparison (less than)
>=	Logical comparison (greater than or equal to)
<=	Logical comparison (less than or equal to)
<>	Logical comparison (not equal to)

You can, of course, use as many operators as you need to perform the desired calculation.

Table 4.3 lists some examples of formulas that use various operators.

TABLE 4.3 Example formulas using operators and their results

Formula	What it does
="Part-"&"23A"	Joins (concatenates) the two text strings to produce Part-23A.
=A1&A2	Concatenates the contents of cell A1 with cell A2. Concatenation works with values as well as text. If cell A1 contains 123 and cell A2 contains 456, this formula would return the text 123456. Note that the result of concatenation is always formatted as text.
=6^3	Raises 6 to the third power (216).
=216^(1/3)	Raises 216 to the power of 1/3. This is mathematically equivalent to calculating the cube root of 216, which is 6.
=A1<A2	Returns TRUE if the value in cell A1 is less than the value in cell A2. Otherwise, it returns FALSE. Logical comparison operators also work with text. If A1 contains Bill and A2 contains Julia, the formula would return TRUE because Bill comes before Julia in alphabetical order.
=A1<=A2	Returns TRUE if the value in cell A1 is less than or equal to the value in cell A2. Otherwise, it returns FALSE.

4

Understanding Operator Precedence in Formulas

When Excel calculates the value of a formula, it uses certain rules to determine the order in which the various parts of the formula are calculated. You need to understand these rules so that your formulas produce accurate results.

Table 4.4 lists the Excel operator precedence. This table shows that exponentiation has the highest precedence (performed first), and logical comparisons have the lowest precedence (performed last).

TABLE 4.4 **Operator precedence in Excel formulas**

Symbol	Operator	Precedence
^	Exponentiation	1
*	Multiplication	2
/	Division	2
+	Addition	3
−	Subtraction	3
&	Concatenation	4
=	Equal to	5
<	Less than	5
>	Greater than	5

You can use parentheses to override Excel's built-in order of precedence. Expressions within parentheses are always evaluated first. As an example, entering the following formula in any cell will result in the answer 49. The parentheses ensure the subtraction is performed before the multiplication:

```
=(10-3)*7
```

If you enter the same formula without the parentheses, Excel computes a different answer. Because multiplication has a higher precedence, the multiplication operation is performed first, giving you the answer −11.

The formula without parentheses looks like this:

```
=10-3*7
```

TIP

It's good practice to use parentheses even when they aren't strictly necessary. Doing so helps to clarify what the formula is intended to do. For example, the following formula makes it perfectly clear that B3 should be multiplied by B4 and the result subtracted from cell B2. Without the parentheses, you would need to remember Excel's order of precedence.

```
=B2-(B3*B4)
```

You can also nest parentheses within formulas—that is, put them inside other parentheses. If you do so, Excel evaluates the most deeply nested expressions first—and then works its way out. Here's an example of a formula that uses nested parentheses:

```
=((B2*C2)+(B3*C3)+(B4*C4))*B6
```

This formula has four sets of parentheses—three sets are nested inside the fourth set. Excel evaluates each nested set of parentheses and then sums the three results. This result is then multiplied by the value in cell B6.

Although the preceding formula uses four sets of parentheses, only the outer set is really necessary in this example. If you understand operator precedence, it should be clear that you can rewrite this formula as follows:

```
=(B2*C2+B3*C3+B4*C4)*B6
```

Note that operators at the same level of precedence, such as multiplication and division, are evaluated from left to right (unless parentheses would indicate a different order).

Every left parenthesis, of course, must have a matching right parenthesis. If you have many levels of nested parentheses, keeping them straight can sometimes be difficult. If the parentheses don't match, Excel displays a message explaining the problem, and it won't let you enter the formula.

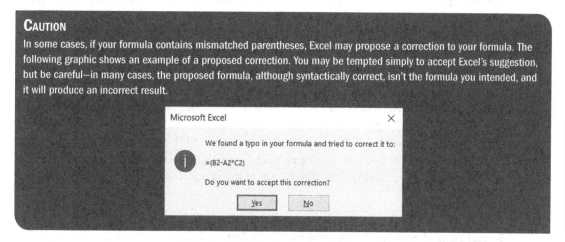

Using Functions in Your Formulas

Many formulas that you create use worksheet functions. These functions enable you to greatly enhance the power of your formulas and perform calculations that are difficult (or even impossible) if you use only the operators discussed previously. For example, you can use the TAN function to calculate the tangent of an angle. You can't do this complicated calculation by using the mathematical operators alone.

Examples of Formulas That Use Functions

A worksheet function can simplify a formula significantly.

Here's an example. To calculate the average of the values in 10 cells (A1:A10) without using a function, you'd have to construct a formula like this:

    =(A1+A2+A3+A4+A5+A6+A7+A8+A9+A10)/10

Not very pretty, is it? Even worse, you would need to edit this formula if you added another cell to the range. Fortunately, you can replace this formula with a much simpler one that uses one of Excel's built-in worksheet functions, AVERAGE:

    =AVERAGE(A1:A10)

The following formula demonstrates how using a function can enable you to perform calculations that are not otherwise possible. Say you need to determine the largest value in a range. A formula can't tell you the answer without using a function. Here's a formula that uses the MAX function to return the largest value in the range A1:D100:

    =MAX(A1:D100)

Functions also can sometimes eliminate manual editing. Assume that you have a worksheet that contains 1,000 names in cells A1:A1000 and the names appear in all-uppercase letters. Your boss sees the listing and informs you that the use of all-uppercase letters is not acceptable; for example, JOHN F. SMITH must now appear as John F. Smith.

With Excel's PROPER function, there's no need to manually correct each of the 1,000 names. You can simply enter the following formula in cell B1, then copy it down to the next 999 rows:

    =PROPER(A1)

Several hours of work can be completed with one Excel function.

One last example should convince you of the power of functions. Suppose you have a worksheet that calculates sales commissions. If the salesperson sold $100,000 or more of product (cell A1), the commission rate is 7.5%; otherwise, the commission rate is 5.0%. You can write a formula using the IF function to automatically calculate the correct commission.

The IF function allows you to build formulas that return a different result based on some logic check. For instance, in this scenario, you could use this:

    =IF(A1<100000,A1*5%,A1*7.5%)

This formula checks the value of cell A1, which contains the sales amount. If this value is less than 100,000, the formula returns cell A1 multiplied by 5%. Otherwise, it returns what's in cell A1 multiplied by 7.5%. This example uses three arguments, separated by commas.

In the next section, we'll go into more detail on the concept of arguments.

Function Arguments

In the preceding examples, you may have noticed that all of the functions used parentheses. The information inside the parentheses is the list of arguments.

Functions vary in the way they use arguments. Depending on what it's designed to do, a function may use one of the following:

- No arguments
- One argument
- A fixed number of arguments
- An indeterminate number of arguments
- Optional arguments

An example of a function that doesn't use an argument is the NOW function, which returns the current date and time. Even if a function doesn't use an argument, you must still provide a set of empty parentheses, like this:

```
=NOW()
```

If a function uses more than one argument, separate each argument with a comma. The examples at the beginning of the chapter used cell references for arguments. Excel is quite flexible when it comes to function arguments, however. An argument can consist of a cell reference, literal values, literal text strings, expressions, and even other functions. Here are some examples of functions that use various types of arguments:

Cell or Range Reference: =SUM(A1:A24)

Literal Value: =SQRT(121)

Literal Text String: =PROPER("john f. smith")

Expression: =SQRT(183+12)

Other Functions: =SQRT(SUM(A1:A24))

4

> **NOTE**
>
> A comma is the list separator character for the U.S. version of Excel. Some other language versions may use a semicolon. The list separator is a Windows setting that can be adjusted in the Windows Control Panel. Simply open the Control Panel in Windows, enter the term **Region** in the Search box, then select the resulting link to access the Region dialog box. You will find the list separator setting by clicking Advanced Settings.

More About Functions

All told, Excel includes more than 450 built-in functions. And if that's not enough, you can download or purchase additional specialized functions from third-party suppliers—and even create your own custom functions (by using Visual Basic for Applications [VBA]) if you're so inclined.

Some users feel a bit overwhelmed by the sheer number of functions, but you'll probably find that you use only a dozen or so on a regular basis. And as you'll see, the Excel Insert Function dialog box (described later in this chapter) makes it easy to locate and insert a function, even if it's not one that you use frequently.

Entering Formulas into Your Worksheets

Every formula must begin with an equals sign to inform Excel that the cell contains a formula rather than text. Excel provides two ways to enter a formula into a cell: manually or by pointing to cell references.

Entering a formula manually starts by clicking the cell where you want your formula to reside. In the selected cell, you type an equals sign (=) followed by the formula. For example, you can enter the following formula in cell C1 to add the contents of cells A1 and B1:

```
=A1+B1
```

As you type, the characters appear in the cell and in the Formula bar. You can, of course, use all of the normal editing keys when entering a formula.

Excel provides additional assistance when you create formulas by displaying a drop-down list that contains function names and range names. The items displayed in the list are determined by what you've already typed.

For example, if you click a cell and type an equals sign (=) followed by the letters SU, you'll see the drop-down list shown in Figure 4.1. If you type an additional letter, the list is shortened to show only the matching functions. To have Excel autocomplete an entry in that list, use the navigation keys to highlight the entry and then press Tab. Notice that highlighting a function in the list also displays a brief description of the function. See the sidebar, "Using Formula AutoComplete," for an example of how this feature works.

FIGURE 4.1

Excel displays a drop-down list when you enter a formula.

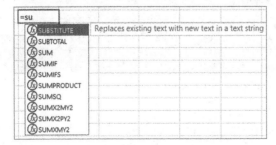

Using Formula AutoComplete

The Formula AutoComplete feature makes entering formulas easier than ever. Simply start typing your formula and Excel will help by presenting you with a list of the possible options and arguments available. In this example, Excel is displaying the options for the SUBTOTAL function. Note in the following graphic, the function name is a hyperlink that, when clicked while you have Internet access, opens a Help task pane providing more information about the function and some basic examples of how the function works.

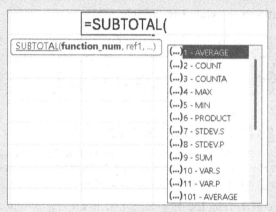

Formula AutoComplete includes the following items (and each type is identified by an icon):

- Excel built-in functions.

- User-defined functions (functions defined by the user through VBA or other methods).

- Defined names (cells or ranges named using the Formulas ⇨ Defined Names ⇨ Define Name command).

- Enumerated arguments that use a value to represent an option (only a few functions use such arguments, and SUBTOTAL is one of them).

- Table structure references (used to identify portions of a table).

Entering Formulas by Pointing

Even though you can enter formulas by typing in the entire formula, Excel provides another method of entering formulas that is generally easier, faster, and less prone to errors. This method still involves some manual typing, but you can simply point to the cell references instead of typing their values manually. For example, to enter the formula =A1+A2 into cell A3, follow these steps:

1. **Select cell A3.**

2. **Type an equals sign (=) to begin the formula.** Notice that Excel displays Enter in the status bar (lower left of your screen).

3. **Press the Up Arrow key twice.** As you press this key, Excel displays a dashed border around cell A1, and the cell reference appears in cell A3 and in the Formula bar. In addition, Excel displays Point in the status bar.

4. **Type a plus sign (+).** A solid color border replaces the dashed border of A1, and Enter reappears in the status bar.

5. **Press the Up Arrow key again.** The dashed border encompasses cell A2 and adds that cell address to the formula.

6. **Press Enter to complete the formula.**

> **TIP**
>
> You can also reference the cells you need in your formulas by either clicking a single cell or dragging across the range of cells needed for your formula.

Pasting Range Names into Formulas

If your formula uses named cells or ranges, you can either type the name in place of the address or choose the name from a list and have Excel insert the name for you automatically. Three ways to insert a name into a formula are available:

- Select the name from the drop-down list. To use this method, you must know at least the first character of the name. When you're entering the formula, type the first character and then select the name from the drop-down list and press Tab.
- Press F3. The Paste Name dialog box appears. Select the name from the list and then click OK (or just double-click the name). Excel enters the name into your formula. If no names are defined, pressing F3 has no effect.
- Click the Use in Formula drop-down on the Formulas tab (Defined Names group). This command is available while you are in edit mode, and it allows you to select from the available range names.

 See Chapter 7, "Working with Excel Ranges," for information about creating names for cells and ranges.

Inserting Functions into Formulas

The easiest way to enter a function into a formula is to select a cell, type the equals sign (=), and then type the first few letters of the function, letting the AutoComplete feature guide you the rest of the way.

Alternatively, you can insert a function using the Function Library group on the Formulas tab on the Ribbon (see Figure 4.2). This method is especially useful if you can't remember which function you need. When entering a formula, click the function category (Financial, Logical, Text, and so on) to get a list of the functions in that category. Click the function that you want, and Excel displays its Function Arguments dialog box. This is where you enter the function's arguments. In addition, you can click the Help on This Function link to learn more about the selected function.

FIGURE 4.2

You can insert a function by selecting it from one of the function categories.

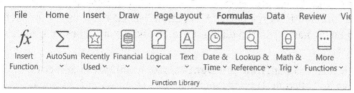

Yet another way to insert a function into a formula is to use the Insert Function dialog box (see Figure 4.3). You can access this dialog box in several ways:

- Choose Formulas ⇨ Function Library ⇨ Insert Function.
- Use the Insert Function command, which appears at the bottom of each drop-down list in the Formulas ⇨ Function Library group.
- Click the Insert Function icon, which is directly to the left of the Formula bar. This button displays *fx*.
- Press Shift+F3.

FIGURE 4.3

The Insert Function dialog box

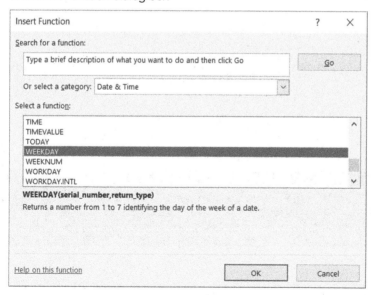

The Insert Function dialog box shows a drop-down list of function categories. Select a category, and the functions in that category are displayed in the list box.

If you're not sure which function you need, you can search for the appropriate function by using the Search For A Function field at the top of the dialog box:

1. **Enter your search terms and click Go.** You get a list of relevant functions. When you select a function from the Select A Function list, Excel displays the function (and its argument names) in the dialog box along with a brief description of what the function does.

2. **When you locate the function you want to use, highlight it and click OK.** Excel then displays its Function Arguments dialog box, as shown in Figure 4.4.

3. **Specify the arguments for the function.** The Function Arguments dialog box will vary depending on the function that you are inserting, and it will show one text box for each of the function's arguments. To use a cell or range reference as an argument, you can enter the address manually or click inside the argument box and then select (i.e., point to) the cell or range in the sheet.

4. **After you specify all the function arguments, click OK.**

FIGURE 4.4

The Function Arguments dialog box

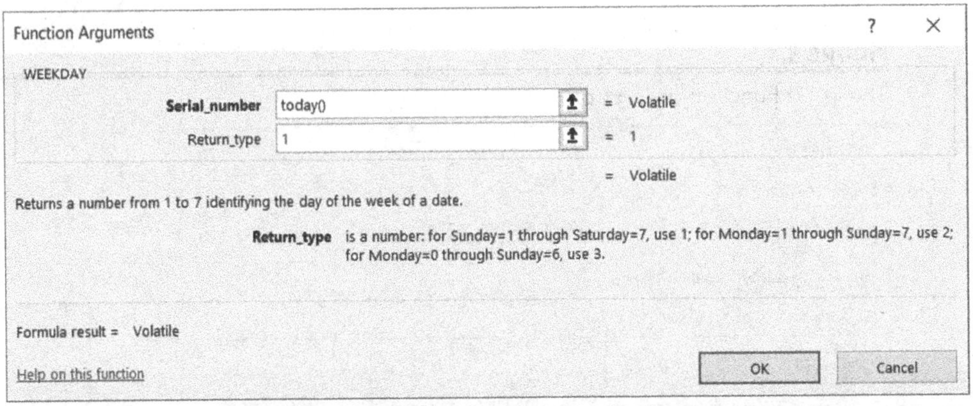

TIP

When you're entering or editing a formula, the space typically occupied by the Name box displays a list of the functions that you've used most recently (if any). You can quickly add any of the functions listed simply by selecting one. After you select a function from this list, Excel will display the Function Arguments dialog box.

Function Entry Tips

Here are some additional tips to keep in mind when you use the Insert Function dialog box to enter functions:

- You can use the Insert Function dialog box to insert a function into an existing formula. Just edit the formula and move the insertion point to the location at which you want to insert the function. Then open the Insert Function dialog box (using any of the methods described earlier) and select the function.

- You can also use the Function Arguments dialog box to modify the arguments for a function in an existing formula. Click the function in the Formula bar and then click the Insert Function button (the *fx* button, to the left of the Formula bar).

- If you change your mind about entering a function, click the Cancel button.

- The number of boxes that you see in the Function Arguments dialog box depends on the number of arguments used in the function you selected. If a function uses no arguments, you won't see any boxes. If the function uses a variable number of arguments (such as the AVERAGE function), Excel adds a new box every time you enter an optional argument. Note that required arguments appear in bold, while optional arguments are not bold.

- As you provide arguments in the Function Arguments dialog box, the value of each argument is displayed to the right of each box.

- A few functions, such as INDEX, have more than one set of arguments depending on what you want that function to do. If you choose such a function, Excel will let you know that function has multiple argument lists and will display another dialog box letting you choose which arguments you want to use.

- As you become familiar with the functions, you can bypass the Insert Function dialog box and type the function name directly. Excel prompts you with argument names as you enter the function.

Editing Formulas

After you enter a formula, you can (of course) edit it. You may need to edit a formula if you make some changes to your worksheet and then have to adjust the formula to accommodate the changes. Or the formula may return an error value, in which case you need to edit the formula to correct the error.

Here are some of the ways to get into cell edit mode:

- Double-click the cell, which enables you to edit the cell contents directly in the cell.
- Press F2, which enables you to edit the cell contents directly in the cell.
- Select the cell that you want to edit and then click in the Formula bar. This enables you to edit the cell contents in the Formula bar.
- If the cell contains a formula that returns an error, Excel will display a small triangle in the upper-left corner of the cell. Activate the cell, and you'll see an error indicator.

Click the error indicator, and you can choose one of the options for correcting the error. (The options will vary according to the type of error in the cell.)

> **TIP**
>
> You can control whether Excel displays these formula error indicators in the Formulas section of the Excel Options dialog box. To display this dialog box, choose File ⇨ Options. If you deselect Enable Background Error Checking, Excel no longer displays these error indicators.

While you're editing a formula, you can select multiple characters either by dragging the pointer over them or by pressing Shift while you use the navigation keys. You may notice that while editing a formula, Excel will color-code the range addresses in the formula. This helps you quickly spot the cells that are used in a formula.

> **TIP**
>
> If you have a formula that you can't seem to edit correctly, you can convert the formula to text and tackle it again later. To convert a formula to text, just remove the initial equals sign (=). When you're ready to try again, type the initial equals sign to convert the cell contents back to a formula.

Using Cell References in Formulas

Imagine you go to cell C1 and enter the formula =A1+B1. Your eyes will see that formula as add the value in A1 to the value in B1. However, Excel doesn't see it that way. Excel translates the formula like this: Take the value in the cell two spaces to the left and add it to the value one space to the left. If you would copy the formula in cell C1 and paste it into cell C2, you'll see the formula in cell C2 would read =A2+B2. In short, Excel doesn't use the actual column and row coordinates you see. Instead, it evaluates cell references in terms of where they are relative to the cell in which the formula resides.

By default, Excel uses what is known as relative references. If you want to ensure that Excel does not adjust cell references when a formula is copied, you can lock the references by turning them into absolute references. This is done by adding a dollar symbol ($) before the column and row reference. For instance, click cell C1 and enter **=$A$1+$B$1**. The dollar symbols ensure that the references in your formula remain fixed (or absolute). If you were to copy the formula in cell C1 and paste it into cell C2, you'll see the formula in cell C2 would remain =$A$1+$B$1.

Using Relative, Absolute, and Mixed References

Excel gives you the flexibility to make any part of your formula a relative reference, absolute reference, or even a mixed reference.

- **Relative Reference:** The row and column references are not locked by dollar symbols ($) and will change when you copy the formula to another cell relative to the cell in which the formula resides.

- **Absolute Reference:** The row and column references are locked by the dollar symbol (`$`) and will not change when you copy the formula. An absolute reference uses two dollar signs in its address: one for the column letter and one for the row number (e.g., `$A$5`).
- **Mixed Reference:** Either the row or the column reference is relative, and the other is absolute. Only one of the address parts is absolute (e.g., `$A4` or `A$4`).

The type of cell reference is important only if you plan to copy the formula to other cells. The following examples illustrate this point.

Figure 4.5 shows a simple worksheet. The formula in cell D2, which multiplies the quantity by the price, is

```
=B2*C2
```

FIGURE 4.5

Copying a formula that contains relative references

D2 | fx | =B2*C2

	A	B	C	D
1	Item	Quantity	Price	Total
2	Chair	4	$125.00	$500.00
3	Desk	4	$695.00	$2,780.00
4	Lamp	3	$39.95	$119.85

This formula uses relative cell references. Therefore, when the formula is copied to the cells below it, the references adjust in a relative manner. For example, the formula in cell D3 is

```
=B3*C3
```

But what if the cell references in D2 contained absolute references, like this?

```
=$B$2*$C$2
```

In this case, copying the formula to the cells below would produce incorrect results. The formula in cell D3 would be the same as the formula in cell D2.

Now we'll extend the example to calculate sales tax, which is stored in cell B7 (see Figure 4.6). In this situation, the formula in cell D2 is

```
=(B2*C2)*$B$7
```

The quantity is multiplied by the price, and the result is multiplied by the sales tax rate stored in cell B7. Notice that the reference to B7 is an absolute reference. When the formula in D2 is copied to the cell below it, cell D3 will contain this formula:

```
=(B3*C3)*$B$7
```

FIGURE 4.6

Formula references to the sales tax cell should be absolute.

D2		×	✓	*fx*	=B2*C2*$B$7	

◢	A	B	C	D	E
1	Item	Quantity	Price	Sales Tax	Total
2	Chair	4	$125.00	$37.50	
3	Desk	4	$695.00		
4	Lamp	3	$39.95		
5					
6					
7	Sales Tax:	7.50%			

Here, the references to cells B2 and C2 were adjusted, but the reference to cell B7 was not, which is exactly what you want because the address of the cell that contains the sales tax never changes.

Figure 4.7 demonstrates the use of mixed references. The formulas in the C3:F7 range calculate the area for various lengths and widths. Here's the formula in cell C3:

=$B3*C$2

FIGURE 4.7

Using mixed cell references

C3		⌄	× ✓	*fx* ⌄	=$B3*C$2	

◢	A	B	C	D	E	F
1				Width		
2			1.0	1.5	2.0	2.5
3		1.0	1.00	1.50	2.00	2.50
4	Length	1.5	1.50	2.25	3.00	3.75
5		2.0	2.00	3.00	4.00	5.00
6		2.5	2.50	3.75	5.00	6.25
7		3.0	3.00	4.50	6.00	7.50

Notice that both cell references are mixed. The reference to cell B3 uses an absolute reference for the column ($B), and the reference to cell C2 uses an absolute reference for the row ($2). As a result, this formula can be copied down and across, and the calculations will be correct. For example, the formula in cell F7 is

=$B7*F$2

If C3 used either absolute or relative references, copying the formula would produce incorrect results.

 A workbook that demonstrates the various types of references is available on this book's website at www.wiley.com/go/excelquickandeasy. The file is named cell references.xlsx.

> **NOTE**
>
> When you copy and paste a formula, Excel will automatically adjust the cell references. However, if you cut and paste a formula, Excel will assume you want to keep the same cell references and will not adjust them.

Changing the Types of Your References

You can enter nonrelative references (that is, absolute or mixed) manually by inserting dollar signs in the appropriate positions of the cell address. Or you can use a handy shortcut: the F4 key. When you've entered a cell reference (by typing it or by pointing), you can press F4 repeatedly to have Excel cycle through all four reference types.

For example, if you enter =A1 to start a formula, pressing F4 converts the cell reference to =$A$1. Pressing F4 again converts it to =A$1. Pressing it again displays =$A1. Pressing it one more time returns to the original =A1. Keep pressing F4 until Excel displays the type of reference that you want.

> **NOTE**
>
> When you name a cell or range, Excel (by default) uses an absolute reference for the name. For example, if you give the name `SalesForecast` to `B1:B12`, the Refers To box in the New Name dialog box lists the reference as `$B$1:$B$12`. If you copy a cell that has a named reference in its formula, the copied formula contains a reference to the original name.

Referencing Cells Outside the Worksheet

Formulas can also refer to cells in other worksheets—and the worksheets don't even have to be in the same workbook. Excel uses a special type of notation to handle these types of references.

Referencing Cells in Other Worksheets

To use a reference to a cell in another worksheet in the same workbook, use this format:

```
=SheetName!CellAddress
```

In other words, precede the cell address with the worksheet name followed by an exclamation point. Here's an example of a formula that uses a cell on the Sheet2 worksheet:

```
=A1*Sheet2!A1
```

This formula multiplies the value in cell A1 on the current worksheet by the value in cell A1 on Sheet2.

4

Referencing Cells in Other Workbooks

To refer to a cell in a different workbook, use this format:

`=[WorkbookName]SheetName!CellAddress`

In this case, the workbook name (in square brackets), the worksheet name, and an exclamation point precede the cell address. The following is an example of a formula that uses a cell reference in the `Sheet1` worksheet in a workbook named `Budget`:

`=[Budget.xlsx]Sheet1!A1`

If the workbook name in the reference includes one or more spaces, you must enclose it (and the sheet name and square brackets) in single quotation marks. For example, here's a formula that refers to a cell on `Sheet1` in a workbook named `Budget For 2022`:

`=A1*'[Budget For 2022.xlsx]Sheet1'!A1`

When a formula refers to cells in a different workbook, the other workbook doesn't have to be open. If the workbook is closed, however, you must add the complete path to the reference so that Excel can find it. Here's an example:

`=A1*'C:\My Documents\[Budget For 2022.xlsx]Sheet1'!A1`

A linked file can also reside on another system that's accessible on your corporate network. The following formula refers to a cell in a workbook in the `files` directory of a computer named `DataServer`:

`='\\DataServer\files\[budget.xlsx]Sheet1'!$D$7`

Moving Beyond Formula Basics

IN THIS CHAPTER

- Using formula variables
- Using advanced formula naming techniques
- Correcting common formula errors
- Getting tips for working with formulas

Creating basic formulas and leveraging the many functions available in Excel suits the needs of many users. Other users, however, may need to create more complex formulas to perform sophisticated calculations. If the latter applies to you, be assured that Excel enables you to take advantage of techniques that streamline your formulas. This chapter introduces how to use variables and naming in formulas, passes along other formula tips, and explains how to troubleshoot common formula errors.

Introducing Formula Variables

As you build formulas, you'll notice it sometimes becomes necessary to repeat the same calculation more than once in a formula. This is often the case when writing nested formulas—formulas that use the results of other functions as arguments.

For instance, the following formula uses a nested IF function to check the result of A1+B1. If the result is less than 50, then "Below Fifty" will be displayed. If the value is greater than 100, then "Above One Hundred" will be displayed. If neither the first nor the second condition is true, then the formulas will display "In Between."

```
=IF(A1+B1<50,"Below Fifty",IF(A1+B1>100,"Above One Hundred","In Between"))
```

You can see Excel has to calculate A1+B1 twice; once to check the first IF condition and once to check the second condition. In this simple example, calculating A1+B1 twice won't bring Excel to a standstill, but the fact is Excel is forced to perform a redundant calculation. In more complex formulas with many nested functions, the need to perform the same calculation over and over can affect performance. In addition to performance considerations, nested calculations can be difficult to read.

In the following sections, you'll discover how formula variables can be leveraged to simplify your formulas and potentially improve performance.

Understanding the *LET* Function

The LET function allows you to create a container of sorts that holds the results of a function or calculation. This container is called a formula variable.

The LET function requires a minimum of three arguments:

- **A name for your variable:** You'll want this name to be a friendly name you can easily recognize and understand. Note that your variable name can't start with a number.
- **A value for your variable:** Once you have a name for your variable, you need to specify the value you want the variable to hold. The name and value combination together make up what is known as a value pair.
- **A formula that uses the variable:** The final argument is a formula expression that uses the variable.

To build a basic LET function, click cell A1 and enter the following:

```
=LET(MyVariable,5*2,MyVariable*10)
```

The result of this formula is 100. It first fills MyVariable with the result of 5*2 (in this case 10), then multiplies MyVariable by 10. This particular formula has one value pair. Again, a value pair is a name and value combination.

The LET function shown here uses two value pairs. MyVariable1, which contains 10 (the result of 5*2), and MyVariable2, which contains 50. The final argument multiplies the variables by 10, resulting in 5000.

```
=LET(MyVariable1,5*2,MyVariable2,50,MyVariable1*MyVariable2*10)
```

> **TIP**
>
> You can use up to 126 value pairs in a single LET function.

> **CAUTION**
>
> When naming variables for your LET function, it's best practice to avoid using named ranges defined in the Name Manager. If you use a name already defined in the Name Manager, LET will effectively ignore and override the named range. Refer to Chapter 7, "Working with Excel Ranges," for information on creating and managing named ranges.

Formula Variables in Action

With the basics under your belt, let's take a moment to witness formula variables in action. Figure 5.1 illustrates two formulas. The first formula in cell C6 is a traditional nested IF statement that evaluates the value of C3/D3. You can see in this first formula that C3/D3 is performed twice.

```
=IF((C3/D3)>1,"Goal Met",IF((C3/D3)<1,"Below Goal","Flat"))
```

FIGURE 5.1

Using the LET function to simplify a nested IF statement

	A	B	C	D	E	
1						
2		Month	Projected	Actual		
3		Jan	4,000	3,255		
4						
5						
6	Nested IF	Goal Met	=IF((C3/D3)>1,"Goal Met",IF((C3/D3)<1,"Below Goal","Flat"))			
7						
8	LET Function	Goal Met	=LET(X,C3/D3,IF(X>1,"Goal Met",IF(X<1,"Below Goal","Flat")))			

Leveraging the LET function allows us to gain efficiency by holding the value of C3/D3 in the variable called X. Excel performs that division only one time and then passes the answer to the rest of the formula.

```
=LET(X,C3/D3,IF(X>1,"Goal Met",IF(X<1,"Below Goal","Flat")))
```

Figure 5.2 demonstrates a more complex SWITCH function that calculates the number of days between the Due Date and Invoice Date then returns text to represent the category of aging days of an invoice. The following formula is listed in cell J5:

```
=SWITCH(TRUE,(I3-H3)>90,"90+",(I3-H3)>30,"31-60",(I3-H3)>0,"")
```

FIGURE 5.2

Using the LET function to simplify a SWITCH statement

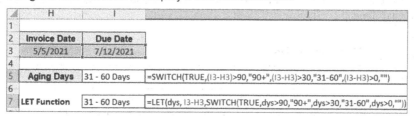

	H	I	J	
1				
2	Invoice Date	Due Date		
3	5/5/2021	7/12/2021		
4				
5	Aging Days	31 - 60 Days	=SWITCH(TRUE,(I3-H3)>90,"90+",(I3-H3)>30,"31-60",(I3-H3)>0,"")	
6				
7	LET Function	31 - 60 Days	=LET(dys, I3-H3,SWITCH(TRUE,dys>90,"90+",dys>30,"31-60",dys>0,""))	

This function calculates the difference in days between the Due Date (cell I3) and the Invoice Date (cell H3) and then returns the appropriate aging category based on the difference in days. Again, not only is this formula difficult to read, but Excel will need to calculate the result of I3-H3 up to three times to fully calculate the correct answer.

5

The improved `LET` function shown in cell J7 (see Figure 5.2) uses the variable `dys` to store the result I3-H3.

```
=LET(dys,I3-H3,SWITCH(TRUE,dys>90,"90+",dys>30,"31-60",dys>0,""))
```

Instead of repeating the initial calculation to get the difference in days, the `dys` variable is filled one time, then passed to the `SWITCH` function.

Correcting Common Formula Errors

Sometimes when you enter a formula, Excel displays a value that begins with a hash mark (#). This is a signal that the formula is returning an error value. You have to correct the formula (or correct a cell that the formula references) to get rid of the error display.

TIP

If the entire cell is filled with hash-mark characters, the column isn't wide enough to display the value. You can either widen the column or change the number format of the cell.

In some cases, Excel won't even let you enter an erroneous formula. For example, the following formula is missing the closing parenthesis:

```
=A1*(B1+C2
```

If you attempt to enter this formula, Excel informs you that you have unmatched parentheses, and it proposes a correction. Often, the proposed correction is accurate, but you can't count on it.

Table 5.1 lists the types of error values that may appear in a cell that has a formula. Formulas may return an error value if a cell to which they refer has an error value. This is known as the *ripple effect*—a single error value can make its way into lots of other cells that contain formulas that depend on that one cell.

TABLE 5.1 Excel error values

Error value	Explanation
#DIV/0!	The formula is trying to divide by zero. Because Excel applies a value of 0 to empty cells, this error also occurs when the formula attempts to divide by a cell that is blank or has a value of 0.
#NAME?	The formula uses a name that Excel doesn't recognize. This can happen if you delete a name that's used in the formula, if you misspell a name used in the formula and then press Enter, or if you have unmatched quotes when using text.
#N/A	The formula is referring (directly or indirectly) to a cell that uses the NA function to signal that data is not available. For instance, the following formula returns an #N/A error if cell A1 is empty: =IF(A1="",NA(),A1). Some lookup functions (for example, VLOOKUP and MATCH) can also return #N/A when they do not find a match.

Error value	Explanation
#NULL!	The formula uses an intersection of two ranges that don't intersect.
#NUM!	A problem with a value exists; for example, you specified a negative number as an argument where a positive number is required.
#REF!	The formula refers to a cell that isn't valid. This can happen if the cell has been deleted from the worksheet.
#VALUE!	The formula includes an argument or operand of the wrong type. (An operand is a value or cell reference that a formula uses to calculate a result.)

Handling Circular References

When you're entering formulas, you may occasionally see a warning message indicating that the formula you just entered will result in a circular reference. A *circular reference* occurs when a formula refers to its own cell—either directly or indirectly. For example, you create a circular reference if you enter =A1+A2+A3 into cell A3 because the formula in cell A3 refers to cell A3. Every time the formula in A3 is calculated, it must be calculated again because A3 has changed. The calculation could go on forever.

When you get the circular reference message after entering a formula, Excel gives you two options:

- Click OK to enter the formula as is.
- Click Help to see a help screen about circular references.

Regardless of which option you choose, Excel displays a message on the left side of the status bar to remind you that a circular reference exists.

> **CAUTION**
>
> Excel won't tell you about a circular reference if the Enable Iterative Calculation setting is selected. You can select this setting in the Formulas section of the Excel Options dialog box. If Enable Iterative Calculation is turned on, Excel performs the circular calculation exactly the number of times specified in the Maximum Iterations field (or until the value changes by less than 0.001 or whatever value is in the Maximum Change field). In a few situations, you may use a circular reference intentionally. In these cases, the Enable Iterative Calculation setting must be selected. However, it's best to keep this setting turned off so that you're warned of circular references. Usually, a circular reference indicates an error that you must correct.

Often, a circular reference is quite obvious and easy to identify and correct. But when a circular reference is indirect (as when a formula refers to another formula that refers to yet another formula that refers to the original formula), it may require a bit of detective work to get to the problem.

Specifying When Formulas Are Calculated

You've probably noticed that Excel calculates the formulas in your worksheet immediately. If you change any cells that the formula uses, Excel displays the formula's new result with no

5

effort on your part. All of this happens when Excel's Calculation mode is set to Automatic. In Automatic Calculation mode (which is the default mode), Excel follows these rules when it calculates your worksheet:

- When you make a change—enter or edit data or formulas, for example—Excel calculates immediately those formulas that depend on new or edited data.
- If Excel is in the middle of a lengthy calculation, it temporarily suspends the calculation when you need to perform other worksheet tasks; it resumes calculating when you're finished with your other worksheet tasks.
- Formulas are evaluated in a natural sequence. In other words, if a formula in cell D12 depends on the result of a formula in cell D24, Excel calculates cell D24 before calculating cell D12.

Sometimes, however, you may want to control when Excel calculates formulas. For example, if you create a worksheet with thousands of complex formulas, you may find that processing can slow to a snail's pace while Excel does its thing. In such a case, set Excel's calculation mode to Manual, which you can do by choosing Formulas ➪ Calculation ➪ Calculation Options ➪ Manual.

When you're working in Manual Calculation mode, Excel displays Calculate in the status bar when you have any uncalculated formulas. You can use the following shortcut keys to recalculate the formulas:

F9: Calculates the formulas in all open workbooks.

Shift+F9: Calculates only the formulas in the active worksheet. Other worksheets in the same workbook aren't calculated.

Ctrl+Alt+F9: Forces a complete recalculation of all formulas.

Ctrl+Alt+Shift+F9: Rebuilds the calculation dependency tree and performs a complete recalculation.

> **NOTE**
>
> Excel's Calculation mode isn't specific to a particular worksheet. When you change the Calculation mode, it affects all open workbooks, not just the active workbook.

Using Advanced Naming Techniques

Using range names can make your formulas easier to understand and modify and even help prevent errors. Dealing with a meaningful name such as AnnualSales is much easier than dealing with a range reference, such as AB12:AB68.

 See Chapter 7 for basic information regarding working with names.

Excel offers a number of advanced techniques that make using names even more useful. We discuss these techniques in the sections that follow. This information is for those who are interested in exploring some of the aspects of Excel that most users don't even know about.

Using Names for Constants

Many Excel users don't realize that you can give a name to an item that doesn't appear in a cell. For example, if formulas in your worksheet use a sales tax rate, you would probably insert the tax rate value into a cell and use this cell reference in your formulas. To make things easier, you would probably also name this cell something similar to SalesTax.

Here's how to provide a name for a value that doesn't appear in a cell:

1. **Choose Formulas ⇨ Defined Names ⇨ Define Name.** The New Name dialog box appears.

2. **Enter the name (in this case, SalesTax) into the Name field.**

3. **Select a scope in which the name will be valid (either the entire workbook or a specific worksheet).**

4. **Click the Refers To text box, delete its contents, and replace the old contents with a value (such as .075).**

5. **(Optional) Use the Comment box to provide a comment about the name.**

6. **Click OK to close the New Name dialog box and create the name.**

You just created a name that refers to a constant rather than a cell or range. Now if you type =SalesTax into a cell that's within the scope of the name, this simple formula returns 0.075—the constant that you defined. You can also use this constant in a formula, such as =A1*SalesTax.

TIP

A constant also can be text. For example, you can define a constant for your company's name.

NOTE

Named constants don't appear in the Name box or in the Go To dialog box. This makes sense because these constants don't reside anywhere tangible. They do appear in the drop-down list that's displayed when you enter a formula. This is handy because you use these names in formulas.

Using Names for Formulas

In addition to creating named constants, you can create named formulas. Like a named constant, a named formula doesn't reside in a cell.

5

You create named formulas the same way that you create named constants—by using the New Name dialog box. For example, you might create a named formula that calculates the monthly interest rate from an annual rate; Figure 5.3 shows an example. In this case, the name MonthlyRate refers to the following formula:

```
=Sheet3!$B$1/12
```

FIGURE 5.3

Excel allows you to name a formula that doesn't exist in a worksheet cell.

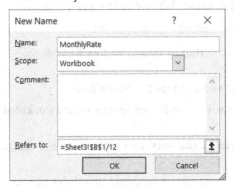

When you use the name MonthlyRate in a formula, it uses the value in B1 divided by 12 on Sheet3. Notice that the cell reference is an absolute reference.

Naming formulas gets more interesting when you use relative references rather than absolute references. When you use the pointing technique to create a formula in the Refers To field of the New Name dialog box, Excel always uses absolute cell references—which is unlike its behavior when you create a formula in a cell.

For example, activate cell B1 on Sheet1 and create the name Cubed for the following formula:

```
=Sheet1!A1^3
```

In this example, the relative reference points to the cell to the left of the cell in which the name is used. Therefore, make certain that cell B1 is the active cell before you open the New Name dialog box; this is important. The formula contains a relative reference. When you use this named formula in a worksheet, the cell reference is always relative to the cell that contains the formula. For example, if you enter =Cubed into cell D12, cell D12 displays the contents of cell C12 raised to the third power. (C12 is the cell directly to the left of cell D12.)

Using Range Intersections

This section describes a concept known as *range intersections* (individual cells that two ranges have in common). Excel uses an intersection operator—a space character—to determine the overlapping references in two ranges. Figure 5.4 shows a simple example.

FIGURE 5.4

You can use a range intersection formula to determine values.

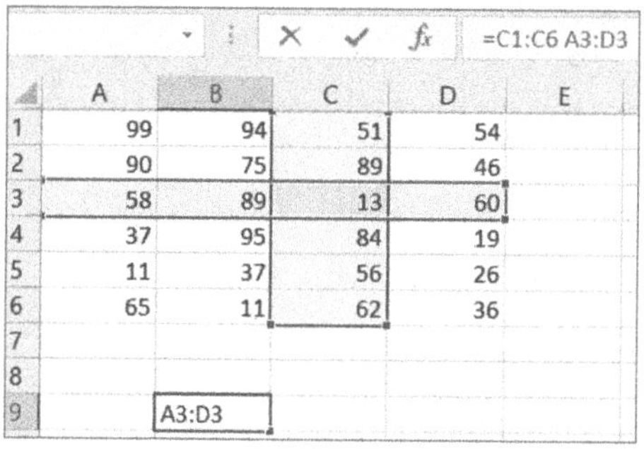

The formula in cell B9 is

    =C1:C6 A3:D3

This formula returns 13, the value in cell C3—that is, the value at the intersection of the two ranges.

The intersection operator is one of three reference operators used with ranges. Table 5.2 lists these operators.

TABLE 5.2 Reference operators for ranges

Operator	What it does
: (colon)	Specifies a range.
, (comma)	Specifies the union of two ranges. This operator combines multiple range references into a single reference.
Space	Specifies the intersection of two ranges. This operator produces cells that are common to two ranges.

The real value of knowing about range intersections is apparent when you use names. Examine Figure 5.5, which shows a table of values. We selected the entire table and then chose Formulas ⇨ Defined Names ⇨ Create From Selection to create names automatically using the top row and the left column.

Excel created the following eight names:

East	=Sheet1!$B$4:$E$4	Quarter3	=Sheet1!$D$2:$D$5
North	=Sheet1!$B$2:$E$2	Quarter1	=Sheet1!$B$2:$B$5
South	=Sheet1!$B$3:$E$3	Quarter2	=Sheet1!$C$2:$C$5
West	=Sheet1!$B$5:$E$5	Quarter4	=Sheet1!$E$2:$E$5

5

FIGURE 5.5

Creating names for all values in a table

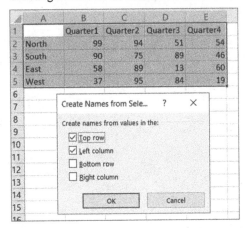

With these names defined, you can create formulas that are easy to read and use. For example, to calculate the total for Quarter 4, just use this formula:

```
=SUM(Quarter4)
```

To refer to a single cell, use the intersection operator. Move to any blank cell and enter the following formula:

```
=Quarter1 West
```

This formula returns the value for the first quarter for the West region. In other words, it returns the value that exists where the Quarter1 range intersects with the West range. Naming ranges in this manner can help you create very readable formulas.

Applying Names to Existing References

When you create a name for a cell or a range, Excel doesn't automatically use the name in place of existing references in your formulas. For example, suppose you have the following formula in cell F10:

```
=A1-A2
```

If you later define a name Income for A1 and Expenses for A2, Excel won't automatically change your formula to =Income-Expenses. Replacing cell or range references with their corresponding names is fairly easy, however.

To apply names to cell references in formulas after the fact, start by selecting the range that you want to modify. Then choose Formulas ➪ Defined Names ➪ Define Name ➪ Apply Names. The Apply Names dialog box appears. Select the names you want to apply by clicking them and then click OK. Excel replaces the range references with the names in the selected cells.

Working With Formulas

In the following sections, we offer a few additional tips and pointers relevant to formulas.

Not Hard-Coding Values

When you create a formula, think twice before you use any specific value in the formula. For example, if your formula calculates a 6.5% sales tax, you may be tempted to enter a formula such as the following:

```
=A1*.065
```

A better approach is to insert the sales tax rate in a cell—and use the cell reference. Or you can define the tax rate as a named constant, using the technique presented earlier in this chapter. Doing so makes modifying and maintaining your worksheet easier. For example, if the sales tax rate changed to 6.75%, you would have to modify every formula that used the old value. If you store the tax rate in a cell, however, you simply change that one cell, and Excel updates all the formulas.

Using the Formula Bar as a Calculator

If you need to perform a quick calculation, you can use the Formula bar as a calculator. For example, enter the following formula but don't press Enter:

```
=(145*1.05)/12
```

If you press Enter, Excel enters the formula into the cell. But because this formula always returns the same result, you may prefer to store the formula's result rather than the formula itself. To do so, press F9 and watch the result appear in the Formula bar. Press Enter to store the result in the active cell. (This technique also works if the formula uses cell references or worksheet functions.)

Making an Exact Copy of a Formula

When you copy a formula, Excel adjusts its cell references when you paste the formula to a different location. Sometimes you may want to make an exact copy of the formula. One way to do this is to convert the cell references to absolute values, but this isn't always desirable. A better approach is to select the formula in Edit mode and then copy it to the Clipboard as text. You can do this in several ways. Here's a step-by-step example of how to make an exact copy of the formula in A1 and copy it to A2:

1. **Double-click A1 (or press F2) to get into Edit mode.**
2. **Drag the mouse to select the entire formula.** You can drag from left to right or from right to left. To select the entire formula with the keyboard, press End, followed by Shift+Home.
3. **Choose Home ➪ Clipboard ➪ Copy (or press Ctrl+C).** This copies the selected text (which will become the copied formula) to the Clipboard.

5

4. **Press Esc to leave Edit mode.**

5. **Select cell A2.**

6. **Choose Home ⇨ Clipboard ⇨ Paste (or press Ctrl+V) to paste the text into cell A2.**

You can also use this technique to copy just part of a formula if you want to use that part in another formula. Just select the part of the formula that you want to copy by dragging the mouse and then use any of the available techniques to copy the selection to the Clipboard. You can then paste the text to another cell.

Formulas (or parts of formulas) copied in this manner won't have their cell references adjusted when they're pasted into a new cell. That's because the formulas are being copied as text, not as actual formulas.

> **TIP**
>
> You can also convert a formula to text by adding an apostrophe (') in front of the equals sign. Then copy the cell as usual and paste it to its new location. Remove the apostrophe from the pasted formula, and it will be identical to the original formula. Don't forget to remove the apostrophe from the original formula.

Converting Formulas to Values

In certain scenarios, you may want to use formulas to get to an answer and then convert those formulas to actual values. For example, if you use the RANDBETWEEN function to create a set of random numbers in cells A1:A20, and you don't want Excel to recalculate those random numbers each time you press Enter, you can convert the formulas to values. Just follow these steps:

1. **Select A1:A20.**

2. **Choose Home ⇨ Clipboard ⇨ Copy (or press Ctrl+C).**

3. **Choose Home ⇨ Clipboard ⇨ Paste Values (V).**

4. **Press Esc to cancel Copy mode.**

Performing Basic Worksheet Operations

IN THIS CHAPTER

- Understanding Excel worksheet basics
- Manipulating the rows and columns

This chapter covers some basic information regarding workbooks, worksheets, and windows. You'll discover tips and techniques to help you take control of your worksheets and help you to work more efficiently.

Learning the Fundamentals of Excel Worksheets

In Excel, each file is called a *workbook*, and each workbook can contain one or more worksheets. You may find it helpful to think of an Excel workbook as a binder and worksheets as pages in the binder. As with a binder, you can view a particular sheet, add new sheets, remove sheets, rearrange sheets, and copy sheets.

A workbook can hold any number of sheets, and these sheets can be either worksheets (sheets consisting of rows and columns) or chart sheets (sheets that hold a single chart). A worksheet is what people usually think of when they think of a spreadsheet.

The following sections describe the operations that you can perform with windows and worksheets.

Working with Excel Windows

Each Excel workbook file that you open is displayed in a window. A window is the operating system's container for that workbook. You can open as many Excel workbooks as necessary at the same time.

Each Excel window has four icons at the right side of its title bar. From left to right, they are Account, Minimize, Maximize (or Restore Down), and Close.

An Excel window can be in one of the following states:

- **Maximized:** Fills the entire screen. To maximize a window, click its Maximize button.

- **Minimized:** Hidden but still open. To minimize a window, click its Minimize button.
- **Restored:** Visible but smaller than the whole screen. To restore a maximized window, click its Restore Down button. To restore a minimized window, click its icon in the Windows taskbar. A window in this state can be resized and moved.

If you work with more than one workbook simultaneously (which is quite common), you need to know how to move, resize, close, and switch among the workbook windows.

Moving and Resizing Windows

To move a window, click and drag its title bar with your mouse. If it's maximized, it will change to a restored state. If it's already in a restored state, it will maintain its current size.

To resize a window, click and drag any of its borders until it's the size that you want it to be. When you position the mouse pointer on a window's border, the mouse pointer changes to a double arrow, which lets you know that you can now click and drag to resize the window. To resize a window horizontally and vertically at the same time, click and drag any of its corners.

If you want all your workbook windows to be visible (that is, not obscured by another window), you can move and resize the windows manually, or you can let Excel do it for you. Choosing View ➪ Window ➪ Arrange All displays the Arrange Windows dialog box, as shown in Figure 6.1. This dialog box has four window arrangement options. Just select the one that you want and click OK. Windows that are minimized aren't affected by this command.

FIGURE 6.1

Use the Arrange Windows dialog box to arrange all open non-minimized workbook windows quickly.

Switching Among Windows

At any given time, one (and only one) workbook window is the active window. The active window accepts your input, and it is the window on which your commands work. The text in the active window's title bar is brighter than that of other windows. To work in a workbook in a different window, you need to make that window active. You can make a different window the active window in several ways:

Click another window if it's visible.

The window you click moves to the top and becomes the active window. This method isn't possible if the current window is maximized unless the other window is on a different monitor.

Press Ctrl+Tab to cycle through all open windows until the window that you want to work with appears on top as the active window.

Pressing Ctrl+Shift+Tab cycles through the windows in the opposite direction.

Press Alt+Tab or Alt+Shift+Tab to cycle through all open windows of all running programs.

Since more recent versions of Excel display each Excel window in its own Windows window, you can use this shortcut key combination to switch between them as you would switch between two programs, like between Excel and Word.

Choose View ⇨ Window ⇨ Switch Windows and select the window that you want from the drop-down list (the active window has a check mark next to it).

This menu can display as many as nine windows. If you have more than nine workbook windows open, choose More Windows (which appears below the nine window names).

Click the corresponding Excel icon in the Windows taskbar.

If there is only one window, this will activate it. If there is more than one window, Windows will display a thumbnail of each and you can click one to activate it.

You might be one of the many people who prefer to do most work with maximized workbook windows, which enables you to see more cells and eliminates the distraction of other workbook windows getting in the way. At times, however, viewing multiple windows is preferred. For example, displaying two windows is more efficient if you need to compare information in two workbooks or if you need to copy data from one workbook to another.

Closing Windows

If you have multiple windows open, you may want to close those windows that you no longer need. Excel offers several ways to close the active window:

- Choose File ⇨ Close.
- Click the Close button (the X icon) on the right side of the workbook window's title bar.
- Press Alt+F4.
- Press Ctrl+W.

When you close a workbook window, Excel checks whether you have made any changes since the last time you saved the file. If you have made changes, Excel prompts you to save the file before it closes the window. If you haven't, the window closes without a prompt from Excel.

Sometimes you will be prompted to save a workbook even if you've made no changes to it. This occurs if your workbook contains any *volatile* functions. Volatile functions recalculate every time the workbook recalculates. For example, if a cell contains =NOW(), you will be prompted to save the workbook because the NOW function updated the cell with the current date and time.

Activating a Worksheet

At any given time, one workbook is the active workbook and one sheet is the active sheet in the active workbook. To activate a different sheet, just click its sheet tab, which is located at the bottom of the workbook window. You also can use the following shortcut keys to activate a different sheet:

- **Ctrl+PgUp** activates the previous sheet if one exists.
- **Ctrl+PgDn** activates the next sheet if one exists.

If your workbook has many sheets, all its tabs may not be visible. Use the sheet tab controls (see Figure 6.2) to scroll the sheet tabs. Clicking the sheet tab controls scrolls one tab at a time, and Ctrl-clicking scrolls to the first or last sheet. The sheet tabs share space with the worksheet's horizontal scrollbar. You also can drag the tab split control (to the left of the horizontal scrollbar) to display more or fewer tabs. Dragging the tab split control simultaneously changes the number of visible tabs and the size of the horizontal scrollbar.

FIGURE 6.2

Use the sheet tab controls to activate a different worksheet or to see additional worksheet tabs.

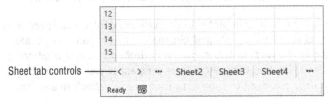

TIP

When you right-click either of the tab scrolling controls, Excel displays a list of all sheets in the workbook. You can quickly activate a sheet by double-clicking it in the list.

Adding a New Worksheet to Your Workbook

Worksheets can be an excellent organizational tool. Instead of placing everything on a single worksheet, you can use additional worksheets in a workbook to separate various workbook elements logically. For example, if you have several products whose sales you track individually, you may want to assign each product to its own worksheet and then use another worksheet to consolidate your results.

Here are four ways to add a new worksheet to a workbook:

- Click the New Sheet button, which is the plus sign icon located to the right of the last visible sheet tab. A new sheet is added after the active sheet.

- Press Shift+F11. A new sheet is added before the active sheet.
- From the Ribbon, choose Home ⇨ Cells ⇨ Insert ⇨ Insert Sheet. A new sheet is added before the active sheet.
- Right-click a sheet tab, choose Insert from the context menu, and select the General tab of the Insert dialog box that appears. Then click the Worksheet icon and click OK. A new sheet is added before the active sheet.

Deleting a Worksheet You No Longer Need

If you no longer need a worksheet or if you want to get rid of an empty worksheet in a workbook, you can delete it in one of two ways:

- Right-click its sheet tab and choose Delete from the context menu.
- Activate the unwanted worksheet and choose Home ⇨ Cells ⇨ Delete ⇨ Delete Sheet.

If the worksheet is not empty, Excel asks you to confirm that you want to delete the sheet (see Figure 6.3).

FIGURE 6.3

Excel's warning that you might be losing some data

> **TIP**
>
> You can delete multiple sheets with a single command by selecting the sheets that you want to delete. To select multiple sheets, press Ctrl while you click the sheet tabs that you want to delete. To select a group of contiguous sheets, click the first sheet tab, press Shift, and then click the last sheet tab (Excel displays the selected sheet names bold and underlined). Then use either method to delete the selected sheets.

> **CAUTION**
>
> When you delete a worksheet, it's gone for good. Deleting a worksheet is one of the few operations in Excel that can't be undone.

Changing the Name of a Worksheet

The default names that Excel uses for worksheets—Sheet1, Sheet2, and so on—are generic and nondescriptive. To make it easier to locate data in a multisheet workbook, you'll want to make the sheet names more descriptive.

These are three ways to change a sheet's name:

- From the Ribbon, choose Home ⇨ Cells ⇨ Format ⇨ Rename Sheet.
- Double-click the sheet tab.
- Right-click the sheet tab and choose Rename.

Excel highlights the name on the sheet tab so that you can edit the name or replace it with a new name. While you're editing a sheet name, all the normal text selection techniques work, such as Home, End, arrow keys, and Shift+arrow keys. Press Enter when you're finished editing and the focus will be back on the active cell.

Sheet names can contain as many as 31 characters, and spaces are allowed. However, there are certain characters you cannot use (see Table 6.1).

TABLE 6.1 Characters you can't use in sheet names

Character	Meaning
:	Colon
/	Slash
\	Backslash
[ ]	Square brackets
?	Question mark
*	Asterisk

Keep in mind that a longer worksheet name results in a wider tab, which takes up more space onscreen. Therefore, if you use lengthy sheet names, you won't be able to see as many sheet tabs without scrolling the tab list.

Changing a Sheet Tab Color

Excel allows you to change the background color of your worksheet tabs. For example, you may prefer to color-code the sheet tabs to make identifying the worksheet's contents easier.

To change the color of a sheet tab, choose Home ⇨ Cells ⇨ Format ⇨ Tab Color, or right-click the tab and choose Tab Color from the context menu. Then select the color from the color palette. You can't change the text color, but Excel will choose a contrasting color to make the text visible. For example, if you make a sheet tab black, Excel will display white text.

If you change a sheet tab's color, the tab shows a gradient from that color to white when the sheet is active. When a different sheet is active, the whole tab appears in the selected color.

Rearranging Your Worksheets

You may want to rearrange the order of worksheets in a workbook. If you have a separate worksheet for each sales region, for example, arranging the worksheets in alphabetical order

6

might be helpful. You can also move a worksheet from one workbook to another and create copies of worksheets, either in the same workbook or in a different workbook.

You can move a worksheet in the following ways:

- Right-click the sheet tab and choose Move Or Copy to display the Move Or Copy dialog box (see Figure 6.4). Use this dialog box to specify the location for the sheet.
- From the Ribbon, choose Home ➪ Cells ➪ Format ➪ Move Or Copy Sheet. This shows the same dialog box as the previous method.
- Click the worksheet tab and drag it to its desired location. When you drag, the mouse pointer changes to a small sheet icon, and a small arrow indicates where the sheet will be placed when you release the mouse button. To move a worksheet to a different workbook by dragging, both workbooks must be visible.

FIGURE 6.4

Use the Move Or Copy dialog box to move or copy worksheets in the same or another workbook.

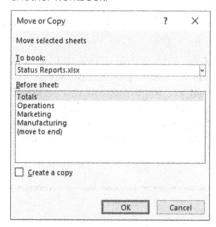

Copying the worksheet is similar to moving it. If you use one of the options that shows the Move Or Copy dialog box, select Create A Copy. To drag and create a copy, hold down the Ctrl key while you drag the worksheet tab. The mouse pointer will change to a small sheet icon with a plus sign on it.

TIP

You can move or copy multiple sheets simultaneously. First, select the sheets by clicking their sheet tabs while holding down the Ctrl key. Then you can move or copy the set of sheets by using the methods just described.

If you move or copy a worksheet to a workbook that already has a sheet with the same name, Excel changes the name to make it unique. For example, Sheet1 becomes Sheet1 (2). You probably want to rename the copied sheet to give it a more meaningful name. (See "Changing the Name of a Worksheet," earlier in this chapter.)

> **NOTE**
>
> When you move or copy a worksheet to a different workbook, any defined names and custom formats are also copied to the new workbook.

Hiding and Unhiding a Worksheet

In some situations, you may want to hide one or more worksheets. Hiding a sheet may be useful if you don't want others to see it or if you just want to get it out of the way. When a sheet is hidden, its sheet tab is also hidden. You can't hide all the sheets in a workbook; at least one sheet must remain visible.

To hide a worksheet, choose Home ⇨ Cells ⇨ Format ⇨ Hide & Unhide ⇨ Hide Sheet, or right-click its sheet tab and choose Hide. The active worksheet (or selected worksheets) will be hidden from view.

To unhide a hidden worksheet, choose Home ⇨ Cells ⇨ Format ⇨ Hide & Unhide ⇨ Unhide Sheet, or right-click any sheet tab and choose Unhide. Excel opens the Unhide dialog box, which lists all hidden sheets. Choose the sheet that you want to redisplay and click OK. You can select multiple sheets from this dialog box by holding down the Ctrl key and clicking the sheets you want to unhide. Hold down the Shift key and click a sheet to select a range of contiguous sheets. When you unhide a sheet, it appears in its previous position among the sheet tabs.

Preventing Sheet Actions

To prevent others from unhiding hidden sheets, inserting new sheets, renaming sheets, copying sheets, or deleting sheets, protect the workbook's structure.

1. Choose Review ⇨ Protect ⇨ Protect Workbook.

2. In the Protect Structure And Windows dialog box, select the Structure option.

3. Provide a password (optional) and click OK.

After you perform these steps, several commands will no longer be available from the Ribbon or when you right-click a sheet tab: Insert, Delete, Rename, Move Or Copy, Tab Color, Hide, and Unhide. Be aware, however, that this is a weak security measure. Cracking this protection feature is relatively easy, especially if you don't add a password.

Working With Rows and Columns

This section discusses worksheet operations that involve complete rows and columns (rather than individual cells). Every worksheet has exactly 1,048,576 rows and 16,384 columns, and these values can't be changed.

> **NOTE**
>
> If you open a workbook that was created in a version of Excel prior to Excel 2007, the workbook is opened in Compatibility Mode. These workbooks have 65,536 rows and 256 columns. If you would like to increase the number of rows and columns, save the workbook as an Excel `.xlsx` file and then reopen it.

Selecting Rows and Columns

Select an entire row by clicking on the row header or using the Shift+spacebar keyboard shortcut. Select an entire column by clicking on the column header or using the Ctrl+spacebar keyboard shortcut.

If you need to select multiple, contiguous rows or columns, click on the header and drag to the adjacent row or column to extend the selection. You can also click on a row or column header, hold down the Shift key, and click on another row or column to extend the selection. To select rows or columns that aren't contiguous, hold down the Ctrl key while you click each header.

Inserting Rows and Columns

Although the number of rows and columns in a worksheet is fixed, you can still insert and delete rows and columns if you need to make room for additional information. These operations don't change the number of rows or columns. Instead, inserting a new row moves down the other rows to accommodate the new row. The last row is simply removed from the worksheet if it's empty. Inserting a new column shifts the columns to the right, and the last column is removed if it's empty.

> **NOTE**
>
> If the last row isn't empty, you can't insert a new row. Similarly, if the last column contains information, Excel doesn't let you insert a new column. In either case, attempting to insert a row or column displays the dialog box shown in Figure 6.5.

FIGURE 6.5

You can't insert a new row or column if it causes nonblank cells to move off the worksheet.

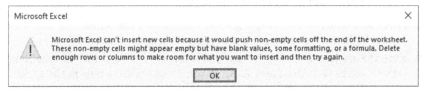

Microsoft Excel   ✕

⚠ Microsoft Excel can't insert new cells because it would push non-empty cells off the end of the worksheet. These non-empty cells might appear empty but have blank values, some formatting, or a formula. Delete enough rows or columns to make room for what you want to insert and then try again.

OK

To insert a new row or rows, use either of these methods:

- Select an entire row or multiple rows by clicking the row numbers in the worksheet border. Right-click and choose Insert from the context menu.
- Select a cell in the row that you want to insert and then choose Home ⇨ Cells ⇨ Insert ⇨ Insert Sheet Rows. If you select multiple cells in the column, Excel inserts additional rows that correspond to the number of cells selected in the column and moves the rows below the insertion down.

To insert a new column or columns, use either of these methods:

- Select an entire column or columns by clicking the column letters in the worksheet border. Right-click and choose Insert from the context menu.
- Select a cell in the column that you want to insert and then choose Home ⇨ Cells ⇨ Insert ⇨ Insert Sheet Columns. If you select multiple cells in the row, Excel inserts additional columns that correspond to the number of cells selected in the row.

You can also insert cells rather than just entire rows or columns. Select the range into which you want to add new cells and then choose Home ⇨ Cells ⇨ Insert ⇨ Insert Cells (or right-click the selection and choose Insert). To insert cells, you must shift the existing cells to the right or down. Therefore, Excel displays the Insert dialog box shown in Figure 6.6 so that you can specify the direction in which you want to shift the cells. Notice that this dialog box also enables you to insert entire rows or columns.

FIGURE 6.6

You can insert partial rows or columns by using the Insert dialog box.

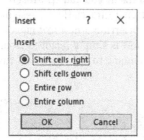

Deleting Rows and Columns

You may also want to delete rows or columns in a worksheet. For example, your sheet may contain old data that is no longer needed, or you may want to remove empty rows or columns.

To delete a row or rows, use either of these methods:

- Select an entire row or multiple rows by clicking the row numbers in the worksheet border. Right-click and choose Delete from the context menu.
- Move the active cell to the row that you want to delete and then choose Home ⇨ Cells ⇨ Delete ⇨ Delete Sheet Rows. If you select multiple cells in the column, Excel deletes all rows in the selection.

To delete a column or columns, use either of these methods:

- Select an entire column or multiple columns by clicking the column letters in the worksheet border. Right-click and choose Delete from the context menu.
- Move the active cell to the column that you want to delete and then choose Home ➪ Cells ➪ Delete ➪ Delete Sheet Columns. If you select multiple cells in the row, Excel deletes all columns in the selection.

If you discover that you accidentally deleted a row or column, select Undo from the Quick Access Toolbar (or press Ctrl+Z) to undo the action.

TIP

You can use the shortcut keys Ctrl + (plus sign) and Ctrl – (minus sign) to insert and delete rows, columns, or cells. If you have an entire row or entire column selected, those shortcuts will insert or delete the entire row or column. If the selection isn't an entire row or column, the Insert dialog box is displayed.

Changing Column Widths and Row Heights

Often, you'll want to change the width of a column or the height of a row. For example, you can make columns narrower to show more information on a printed page. Or you may want to increase row height to create a "double-spaced" effect.

Excel provides several ways to change the widths of columns and the height of rows.

Changing Column Widths

Column width is measured in terms of the number of characters of a monospaced font that will fit into the cell's width. By default, each column's width is 8.43 units, which equates to 64 pixels (px).

TIP

If hash symbols (#) fill a cell that contains a numerical value, the column isn't wide enough to accommodate the information in the cell. Widen the column to solve the problem.

Before you change the column width, you can select multiple columns so that the width will be the same for all selected columns. To select multiple columns, either click and drag in the column border or press Ctrl while you select individual columns. To select all columns, click the button where the row and column headers intersect. You can change column widths by using any of the following techniques:

- Drag the right-column border with the mouse until the column is the desired width.
- Choose Home ➪ Cells ➪ Format ➪ Column Width and enter a value in the Column Width dialog box.

- Choose Home ➪ Cells ➪ Format ➪ AutoFit Column Width to adjust the width of the selected column so that the widest entry in the column fits. Instead of selecting an entire column, you can just select cells in the column, and the column is adjusted based on the widest entry in your selection.
- Double-click the right border of a column header to set the column width automatically to the widest entry in the column.

TIP

To change the default width of all columns, choose Home ➪ Cells ➪ Format ➪ Default Width. This command displays a dialog box into which you enter the new default column width. All columns that haven't been previously adjusted take on the new column width.

CAUTION

After you manually adjust a column's width, Excel will no longer automatically adjust the column to accommodate longer numerical entries. If you enter a long number that displays as hash symbols (#), you need to change the column width manually.

Changing Row Heights

Row height is measured in points (a standard unit of measurement in the printing trade—72 pts is equal to 1 inch). The default row height using the default font is 15 pts, or 20 pixels (px).

The default row height can vary, depending on the font defined in the Normal style. In addition, Excel automatically adjusts row heights to accommodate the tallest font in the row. So, if you change the font size of a cell to 20 pts, for example, Excel makes the row taller so that the entire text is visible.

You can set the row height manually, however, by using any of the following techniques. As with columns, you can select multiple rows:

- Drag the lower row border with the mouse until the row is the desired height.
- Choose Home ➪ Cells ➪ Format ➪ Row Height and enter a value (in points) in the Row Height dialog box.
- Double-click the bottom border of a row to set the row height automatically to the tallest entry in the row. You can also choose Home ➪ Cells ➪ Format ➪ AutoFit Row Height for this task.

Changing the row height is useful for spacing out rows and is almost always preferable to inserting empty rows between lines of data.

Hiding Rows and Columns

In some cases, you may want to hide rows or columns. Hiding rows and columns may be useful if you don't want users to see particular information or if you need to print a report that summarizes the information in the worksheet without showing all the details.

To hide rows in your worksheet, select the row or rows that you want to hide by clicking in the row header on the left. Then right-click and choose Hide from the context menu. Or you can use the commands on the Home ⇨ Cells ⇨ Format ⇨ Hide & Unhide menu.

To hide columns, select the column or columns that you want to hide. Then right-click and choose Hide from the context menu. Or you can use the commands on the Home ⇨ Cells ⇨ Format ⇨ Hide & Unhide menu.

> **TIP**
>
> You can also drag the row or column's border to hide the row or column. You must drag the border in the row or column heading. Drag the bottom border of a row upward or the right border of a column to the left.

A hidden row is actually a row with its height set to zero. Similarly, a hidden column has a column width of zero. When you use the navigation keys to move the active cell, cells in hidden rows or columns are skipped. In other words, you can't use the navigation keys to move to a cell in a hidden row or column.

Notice, however, that Excel displays a narrow column heading for hidden columns and a narrow row heading for hidden rows. You can click and drag the column heading to make the column wider—and make it visible again. For a hidden row, click and drag the small row heading to make the row visible.

Another way to unhide a row or column is to choose Home ⇨ Editing ⇨ Find & Select ⇨ Go To (or use one of its two shortcut keys: F5 or Ctrl+G) to select a cell in a hidden row or column. For example, if column A is hidden, you can press F5 and go to cell A1 (or any other cell in column A) to move the active cell to the hidden column. Then you can choose Home ⇨ Cells ⇨ Format ⇨ Hide & Unhide ⇨ Unhide Columns.

Working with Excel Ranges

IN THIS CHAPTER

- Understanding Excel cells and ranges
- Selecting cells and ranges
- Copying or moving ranges
- Using names to work with ranges

Most of the work you do in Excel involves cells and ranges. Understanding how best to manipulate cells and ranges will save you time and effort. This chapter discusses a variety of techniques that are essential for Excel users.

Understanding Cells and Ranges

A *cell* is a single element in a worksheet that can hold a value, some text, or a formula. A cell is identified by its address, which consists of its column letter and row number. For example, cell D9 is the cell in the fourth column and the ninth row.

A group of one or more cells is called a *range*. You designate a range address by specifying its upper-left cell address and its lower-right cell address, separated by a colon.

Here are some examples of range addresses:

C24	A range that consists of a single cell.
A1:B1	Two cells that occupy one row and two columns.
A1:A100	100 cells in column A.
A1:D4	16 cells (four rows by four columns).
C1:C1048576	An entire column of cells; this range also can be expressed as C:C.
A6:XFD6	An entire row of cells; this range also can be expressed as 6:6.
A1:XFD1048576	All cells in a worksheet. This range also can be expressed as either A:XFD or 1:1048576.

Selecting Ranges

To perform an operation on a range of cells in a worksheet, you must first select the range. For example, if you want to make the text bold for a range of cells, you must select the range and then choose Home ➪ Font ➪ Bold (or press Ctrl+B).

When you select a range, the cells appear highlighted. The exception is the active cell, which remains its normal color. Figure 7.1 shows an example of a selected range (A4:D8) in a worksheet. Cell A4, the active cell, is in the selected range but not highlighted.

FIGURE 7.1

When you select a range, it appears highlighted, but the active cell within the range is not highlighted.

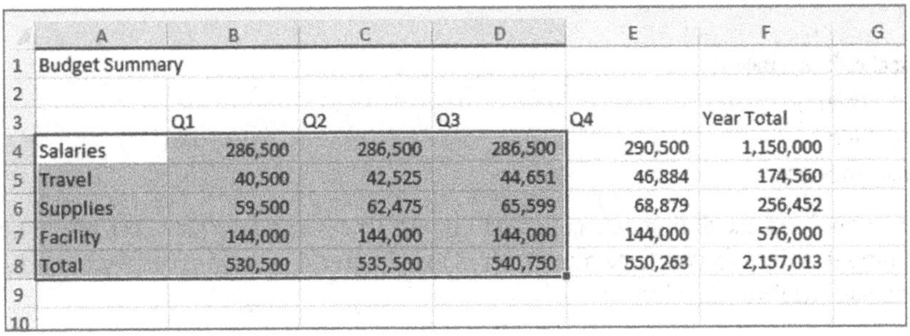

	A	B	C	D	E	F	G
1	Budget Summary						
2							
3		Q1	Q2	Q3	Q4	Year Total	
4	Salaries	286,500	286,500	286,500	290,500	1,150,000	
5	Travel	40,500	42,525	44,651	46,884	174,560	
6	Supplies	59,500	62,475	65,599	68,879	256,452	
7	Facility	144,000	144,000	144,000	144,000	576,000	
8	Total	530,500	535,500	540,750	550,263	2,157,013	
9							
10							

You can select a range in several ways:

- Left-click and drag over the range. If you drag to the end of the window, the worksheet will scroll.
- Press the Shift key while you use the navigation keys.
- Click the top-left cell of the range and press the Shift key while you click the bottom-right cell. This works with any corners of the range. Make one corner active and press Shift while selecting the opposite corner.
- Press F8 to enter Extend Selection mode (Extend Selection appears in the status bar). In this mode, click the lower-right cell of the range or use the navigation keys to extend the range. Press F8 again to exit Extend Selection mode.
- Type the cell or range address into the Name box (located to the left of the Formula bar) and press Enter. Excel selects the cell or range that you specified.
- Choose Home ➪ Editing ➪ Find & Select ➪ Go To (or press F5 or Ctrl+G) and enter a range's address manually in the Go To dialog box. When you click OK, Excel selects the cells in the range that you specified.

> **TIP**
>
> While you're selecting a range that contains more than one cell, Excel displays the number of rows and columns in your selection in the Name box (which is to the left of the Formula bar). When you finish making the selection, the Name box reverts to showing the address of the active cell.

Selecting Complete Rows and Columns

Often, you'll need to select an entire row or column. For example, you may want to apply the same numeric format or the same alignment options to an entire row or column. You can select entire rows and columns in several ways, including the following:

- Click the row or column header to select a single row or column or click and drag for multiple rows or columns.
- To select multiple (nonadjacent) rows or columns, click the first row or column header and then hold down the Ctrl key while you click the additional row or column header that you want.
- Press Ctrl+spacebar to select the column(s) of the currently selected cells. Press Shift+spacebar to select the row(s) of the currently selected cells.

TIP

Press Ctrl+A to select all cells in the worksheet, which is the same as selecting all rows and all columns. If the active cell is within a contiguous range, Ctrl+A will just select that range. In that case, press Ctrl+A again to select all the cells in the worksheet. You can also click the area at the intersection of the row and column headers to select all cells.

Selecting Noncontiguous Ranges

Most of the time, the ranges that you select are contiguous—a single rectangle of cells. Excel also enables you to work with noncontiguous ranges, which consist of two or more ranges (or single cells) that aren't necessarily adjacent to each other. Selecting noncontiguous ranges is also known as a *multiple selection*. If you want to apply the same formatting to cells in different areas of your worksheet, one approach is to make a multiple selection. When the appropriate cells or ranges are selected, the formatting that you select is applied to all of them. Figure 7.2 shows a noncontiguous range selected in a worksheet. Three ranges are selected: B4:B8, D4:D8, and F4:F8.

FIGURE 7.2

Excel enables you to select noncontiguous ranges.

	A	B	C	D	E	F	G
1	Budget Summary						
2							
3		Q1	Q2	Q3	Q4	Year Total	
4	Salaries	286,500	286,500	286,500	290,500	1,150,000	
5	Travel	40,500	42,525	44,651	46,884	174,560	
6	Supplies	59,500	62,475	65,599	68,879	256,452	
7	Facility	144,000	144,000	144,000	144,000	576,000	
8	Total	530,500	535,500	540,750	550,263	2,157,013	
9							
10							

You can select a noncontiguous range in the same ways that you select a contiguous range with a few minor differences. Instead of simply clicking and dragging for contiguous ranges, after you select the first range, hold down the Ctrl key while you click and drag to select additional ranges. If you're selecting a range using the arrow keys, select the first range, then press Shift+F8 to enter Add Or Remove Selection mode (that term will appear in the status bar). Use the arrow keys to move to the next area. If it's a single cell, press Shift+F8 again or Esc to exit Add Or Remove Selection mode. If it's a multicell range, Excel will kick you out of Add Or Remove Selection mode automatically. To add another area, repeat the process starting with pressing Shift+F8. Anywhere you type the range manually, such as in the Name box or the Go To dialog box, simply separate the noncontiguous ranges with a comma. For example, typing **B4:B8,D4:D8,F4:F8** will select the noncontiguous ranges shown in Figure 7.2.

> **NOTE**
>
> Noncontiguous ranges differ from contiguous ranges in several important ways. One major difference is that you can't use drag-and-drop methods (described later) to move or copy noncontiguous ranges.

Selecting Multisheet Ranges

In addition to two-dimensional ranges on a single worksheet, ranges can extend across multiple worksheets to be three-dimensional ranges.

Suppose you have a workbook set up to track budgets. One approach is to use a separate worksheet for each department, making it easy to organize the data. You can click a sheet tab to view the information for a particular department.

Figure 7.3 shows a simplified example. The workbook has four sheets: Totals, Operations, Marketing, and Manufacturing. The sheets are laid out identically. The only difference is the values. The Totals sheet contains formulas that compute the sum of the corresponding items in the three departmental worksheets.

 This workbook, named `budget.xlsx`, is available on this book's website at `www.wiley.com/go/ excelquickandeasy`.

Assume that you want to apply formatting to the sheets—for example, to make the column headings bold with background shading. One (albeit not-so-efficient) approach is to format the cells in each worksheet separately. A better technique is to select a multisheet range and format the cells in all the sheets simultaneously. The following is a step-by-step example of multisheet formatting using the workbook shown in Figure 7.3:

1. **Activate the Totals worksheet by clicking its tab.**

2. **Select the range B3:F3.**

3. **Press Shift and click the Manufacturing sheet tab.** This step selects all worksheets between the active worksheet (Totals) and the sheet tab that you click—in essence, a three-dimensional range of cells (see Figure 7.4). When multiple sheets are selected,

the workbook window's title bar displays Group to remind you that you've selected a group of sheets and that you're in Group mode.

4. **Choose Home ⇨ Font ⇨ Bold and then choose Home ⇨ Font ⇨ Fill Color to apply a colored background.** Excel applies the formatting to the selected range across the selected sheets.

5. **Click one of the other sheet tabs.** This step selects the sheet and cancels Group mode; Group is no longer displayed in the title bar.

FIGURE 7.3

The worksheets in this workbook are laid out identically.

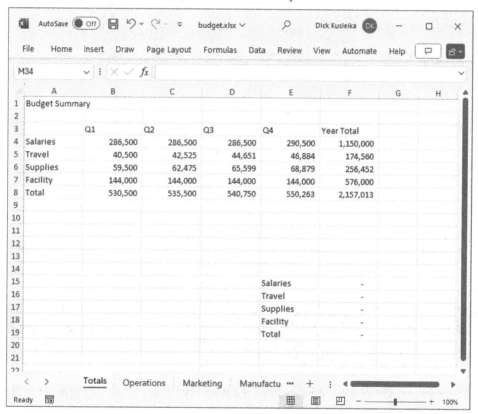

When a workbook is in Group mode, any changes that you make to cells in one worksheet also apply to the corresponding cells in all the other grouped worksheets. You can use this to your advantage when you want to set up a group of identical worksheets because any labels, data, formatting, or formulas you enter are automatically added to the same cells in all the grouped worksheets.

FIGURE 7.4

In Group mode, you can work with a three-dimensional range of cells that extends across multiple worksheets.

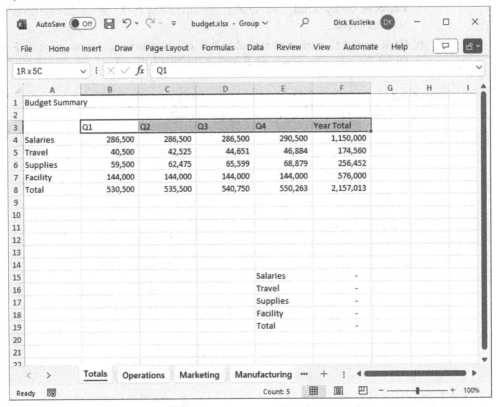

In general, selecting a multisheet range is a simple two-step process: Select the range in one sheet and then select the worksheets to include in the range. To select a group of contiguous worksheets, select the first worksheet in the group and then press Shift and click the sheet tab of the last worksheet that you want to include in the selection. To select individual worksheets, select one of the worksheets in the group and then press Ctrl and click the sheet tab of each additional worksheet that you want to select. If all the worksheets in a workbook aren't laid out the same, you can skip the sheets that you don't want to format. When you make the selection, the sheet tabs of the selected sheets display in bold with underlined text, and Excel displays Group in the title bar.

> **TIP**
>
> To select all sheets in a workbook, right-click any sheet tab and choose Select All Sheets from the context menu.

> **CAUTION**
>
> When sheets are grouped, you are making changes to sheets you can't see. Before you group sheets, be sure you understand what changes you intend to make and how that will affect all the sheets in the group. When you're done, don't forget to ungroup the sheets by selecting a sheet outside the group or selecting Ungroup Sheets from the tab's context menu. You can overwrite data on the other sheets if you start typing on the active sheet while in Group mode.

Selecting Similar Cells

As you use Excel, you may need to select cells in your worksheets that have something in common. For example, you might want to select every cell that contains a formula. Or you might want to select all the cells within a certain range that are blank. Excel provides an easy way to locate these and many other special types of cells: Select a range and choose Home ⇨ Editing ⇨ Find & Select ⇨ Go To Special to display the Go To Special dialog box, as shown in Figure 7.5.

FIGURE 7.5

Use the Go To Special dialog box to select specific types of cells.

After you make your choice in the dialog box and click OK, Excel selects the qualifying subset of cells in the current selection. Often, this subset of cells is a multiple selection. If no cells qualify, Excel lets you know with the message No cells were found.

TIP

If you bring up the Go To Special dialog box with only one cell selected, Excel bases its selection on the entire used area of the worksheet. Otherwise, the selection is based on the selected range.

Table 7.1 offers a description of the options available in the Go To Special dialog box.

TABLE 7.1   Go To Special options

Option	What it does
Notes	Selects the cells that contain a note.
Constants	Selects all nonempty cells that don't contain formulas. Use the check boxes under the Formulas option to choose which types of nonformula cells to include.
Formulas	Selects cells that contain formulas. Qualify this by selecting the type of result: numbers, text, logical values (TRUE or FALSE), or errors.
Blanks	Selects all empty cells. If a single cell is selected when the dialog box is displayed, this option selects the empty cells in the used area of the worksheet.
Current Region	Selects a rectangular range of cells around the active cell. This range is determined by surrounding blank rows and columns. You can also press Ctrl+Shift+*.
Current Array	Selects the entire array.
Objects	Selects all embedded objects on the worksheet, including charts and graphics.
Row Differences	Analyzes the selection and selects cells that are different from other cells in each row.
Column Differences	Analyzes the selection and selects the cells that are different from other cells in each column.
Precedents	Selects cells that are referred to in the formulas in the active cell or selection (limited to the active sheet). You can select either direct precedents or precedents at all levels.
Dependents	Selects cells with formulas that refer to the active cell or selection (limited to the active sheet). You can select either direct dependents or dependents at all levels.
Last Cell	Selects the bottom-right cell in the worksheet that contains data or formatting. For this option, the entire worksheet is examined, even if a range is selected when Excel displays the dialog box.
Visible Cells Only	Selects only visible cells in the selection. This option is useful when dealing with a filtered list or a table.

Option	What it does
Conditional Formats	Selects cells that have a conditional format applied (by choosing Home ⇨ Styles ⇨ Conditional Formatting). The All option selects all such cells. The Same option selects only the cells that have the same conditional formatting as the active cell.
Data Validation	Selects cells that are set up for data entry validation (by choosing Data ⇨ Data Tools ⇨ Data Validation). The All option selects all such cells. The Same option selects only the cells that have the same validation rules as the active cell.

TIP

When you select an option in the Go To Special dialog box, be sure to note which suboptions become available. The placement of these suboptions can be misleading. For example, when you select Constants, the suboptions under Formulas become available to help you further refine the results. Likewise, the suboptions under Dependents also apply to Precedents, and those under Data Validation also apply to Conditional Formats.

Selecting Cells by Searching

Another way to select cells is to choose Home ⇨ Editing ⇨ Find & Select ⇨ Find (or press Ctrl+F), which allows you to select cells by their contents. The Find And Replace dialog box is shown in Figure 7.6. This figure illustrates additional options that are available when you click the Options button.

FIGURE 7.6

The Find And Replace dialog box, with its options displayed

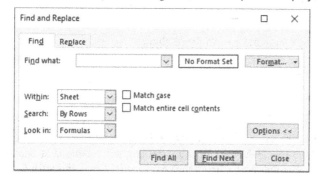

Enter the text you're looking for; then click Find All. The dialog box expands to display all the cells that match your search criteria. For example, Figure 7.7 shows the dialog box after Excel has located all cells that contain the text *travel*. You can click an item in the list, and the screen will scroll so that you can view the cell in context. To select all the cells in the list, first select any single item in the list. Then press Ctrl+A to select them all. You are limited to only selecting cells on the active sheet using this method.

FIGURE 7.7

The Find And Replace dialog box, with its results listed

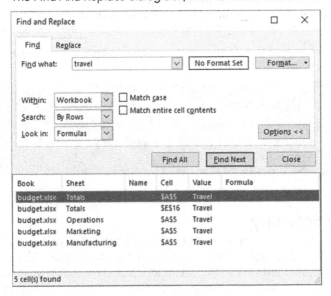

> **NOTE**
> The Find And Replace dialog box allows you to return to the worksheet without dismissing the dialog box.

The Find And Replace dialog box supports two wildcard characters:

?	Matches any single character
*	Matches any number of characters

Wildcard characters also work with values when the Match Entire Cell Contents option is selected. For example, searching for 3* locates all cells that contain a value that begins with 3. Searching for 1?9 locates all three-digit entries that begin with 1 and end with 9. Searching for *00 locates values that end with two zeros.

> **TIP**
>
> To search for a question mark or an asterisk, precede the character with a tilde (~). For example, the following search string finds the text `*NONE*`:
>
> `~*NONE~*`
>
> If you need to search for the tilde character, use two tildes.

If your searches don't seem to be working correctly, double-check these three options:

- **Match Case:** If this option is selected, the case of the text must match exactly. For example, searching for `smith` does not locate `Smith`.
- **Match Entire Cell Contents:** If this option is selected, a match occurs if the cell contains only the search string (and nothing else). For example, searching for `Excel` doesn't locate a cell that contains `Microsoft Excel`. When using wildcard characters, an exact match is not required.
- **Look In:** This drop-down list has four options: Values, Formulas, Notes, and Comments. The Formulas option looks only at the text that makes up the formula or the contents of the cell if there is no formula. The Values option looks at the cell value and the results, not the text, of the formula. If, for example, Formulas is selected, searching for `900` doesn't find a cell that contains the formula `=899+1` but will find a cell with a value of `900`. The Values option will find both of those cells.

Copying or Moving Ranges

As you create a worksheet, you may find it necessary to copy or move information from one location to another. Excel makes copying or moving ranges of cells easy. Here are some common things that you might do:

- Copy a cell to another location.
- Copy a cell to a range of cells. The source cell is copied to every cell in the destination range.
- Copy a range to another range.
- Move a cell or range of cells to another location.

The primary difference between copying and moving a range is the effect of the operation on the source range. When you copy a range, the source range is unaffected. When you move a range, the contents are removed from the source range.

> **NOTE**
>
> Copying a cell normally copies the cell's contents, any formatting that is applied to the original cell (including conditional formatting and data validation), the cell note (if it has one), and the cell comment (if it has one). When you copy a cell that contains a formula, the cell references in the copied formula are changed automatically to be relative to their new destination.

Copying or moving consists of two steps (although shortcut methods are available):

1. Select the cell or range you want to copy (the source range) and copy it to the Clipboard. To move the range instead of copying it, cut the range instead of copying it.

2. Select the cell or range that will hold the copy (the destination range) and paste the Clipboard contents.

> **CAUTION**
>
> When you paste information, Excel overwrites any cells that get in the way without warning you. If you find that pasting overwrote some essential cells, choose Undo from the Quick Access Toolbar (or press Ctrl+Z).

> **CAUTION**
>
> When you copy a cell or range, Excel surrounds the copied area with an animated, dashed border. As long as that border remains visible, the copied information is available for pasting. If you press Esc to cancel the border, Excel removes the information from the Clipboard.

Because copying (or moving) is used so often, Excel provides many different methods. We discuss each method in the following sections. Copying and moving are similar operations, so we point out only important differences between the two.

Copying by Using Ribbon Commands

Choosing Home ➪ Clipboard ➪ Copy transfers a copy of the selected cell or range to the Windows Clipboard and the Office Clipboard. After performing the copy part of this operation, select the destination cell and choose Home ➪ Clipboard ➪ Paste.

Instead of choosing Home ➪ Clipboard ➪ Paste, you can just select the destination cell and press Enter. If you use this technique, Excel removes the copied information from the Clipboard so that it can't be pasted again.

If you're copying a range, you don't need to select an entire same-sized range before you click the Paste button. You only need to select the upper-left cell in the destination range.

> **TIP**
>
> The Home ➪ Clipboard ➪ Paste control contains a drop-down arrow that, when clicked, gives you additional paste option icons. The paste preview icons are explained later in this chapter (see "Pasting in Special Ways").

About the Office Clipboard

Whenever you cut or copy information from a Windows program, Windows stores the information on the Windows Clipboard, which is an area of your computer's memory. Each time that you cut or copy information, Windows replaces the information previously stored on the Clipboard with the new information that you cut or copied. The Windows Clipboard can store data in a variety of formats. Because Windows manages information on the Clipboard, it can be pasted to other Windows applications, regardless of where it originated.

Microsoft Office has its own Clipboard (the Office Clipboard), which is available only in Office programs. To view or hide the Office Clipboard, click the dialog box launcher in the bottom-right corner of the Home ⇨ Clipboard group.

You can find out more about this feature (including an important limitation) in "Using the Office Clipboard to Paste," later in this chapter.

7

Copying by Using Context Menu Commands

If you prefer, you can use the following context menu commands for copying and pasting:

- Right-click the range and choose Copy (or Cut) from the context menu to copy the selected cells to the Clipboard.
- Right-click and choose Paste from the context menu to paste the Clipboard contents to the selected cell or range.

For more control over how the pasted information appears, right-click the destination cell and use one of the Paste icons in the context menu (see Figure 7.8).

Instead of using Paste, you can just activate the destination cell and press Enter. If you use this technique, Excel removes the copied information from the Clipboard so that it can't be pasted again.

Copying by Using Shortcut Keys

The copy and paste operations also have shortcut keys associated with them:

- Ctrl+C copies the selected cells to both the Windows Clipboard and the Office Clipboard.
- Ctrl+X cuts the selected cells to both the Windows Clipboard and the Office Clipboard.
- Ctrl+V pastes the Windows Clipboard contents to the selected cell or range.

TIP

These are standard key combinations used by many other Windows applications.

FIGURE 7.8

The Paste icons on the context menu provide more control over how the pasted information appears.

Using Paste Options Buttons When Inserting and Pasting

Some cell and range operations—specifically inserting, pasting, and filling cells by dragging—result in the display of Paste Options buttons. For example, if you copy a range and then paste it to a different location using Home ➪ Clipboard ➪ Paste, a drop-down list of options appears at the lower right of the pasted range. Click the list (or press Ctrl), and you see options similar to those under the Paste control on the Ribbon. These options enable you to specify how the data should be pasted, such as values only or formatting only. In this case, using the Paste Options buttons is an alternative to using options in the

Paste Special dialog box. (Read more about Paste Special in the upcoming section "Using the Paste Special dialog box.")

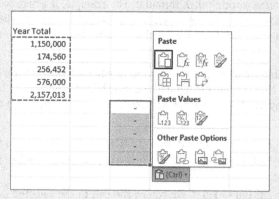

To disable this feature, choose File ➪ Options and select the Advanced tab. Deselect the two options Show Paste Options Button When Content Is Pasted and Show Insert Options Buttons.

Copying or Moving by Using Drag-and-Drop

Excel also enables you to copy or move a cell or range by dragging. Unlike other methods of copying and moving, dragging and dropping does not place any information on either the Windows Clipboard or the Office Clipboard.

CAUTION

The drag-and-drop method of moving does offer one advantage over the cut-and-paste method: Excel warns you if a drag-and-drop move operation will overwrite existing cell contents. Oddly, you do not get a warning if a drag-and-drop copy operation will overwrite existing cell contents.

To move using drag-and-drop, select the cell or range that you want to move and move the mouse to one of the selection's borders. The mouse pointer will change to a northwest arrow with a four-sided arrow. Drag the selection to the new location and release the mouse button.

Copying using drag-and-drop works the same way except that you press Ctrl before dragging. When you press Ctrl, the mouse pointer changes from the four-sided arrow to indicate a move to a northwest arrow with a small plus sign. The original selection remains behind, and Excel makes a new copy when you release the mouse button.

TIP

If the mouse pointer doesn't turn into an arrow when you point to the border of a cell or range, you need to make a change to your settings. Choose File ➪ Options to display the Excel Options dialog box, select the Advanced tab, and select the option Enable Fill Handle And Cell Drag-And-Drop.

Copying to Adjacent Cells

Often, you need to copy a cell to an adjacent cell or range. This type of copying is quite common when you're working with formulas. For example, if you're working on a budget, you might create a formula to add the values in column B. You can use the same formula to add the values in the other columns. Rather than reenter the formula, you can copy it to the adjacent cells.

Excel provides additional options for copying to adjacent cells. To use these commands, activate the cell that you're copying and extend the cell selection to include the cells to which you're copying. Then issue the appropriate command from the following list for one-step copying:

- Home ⇨ Editing ⇨ Fill ⇨ Down (or Ctrl+D) copies the cell to the selected range below.
- Home ⇨ Editing ⇨ Fill ⇨ Right (or Ctrl+R) copies the cell to the selected range to the right.
- Home ⇨ Editing ⇨ Fill ⇨ Up copies the cell to the selected range above.
- Home ⇨ Editing ⇨ Fill ⇨ Left copies the cell to the selected range to the left.

None of these commands places information on either the Windows Clipboard or the Office Clipboard.

TIP

You also can use AutoFill to copy to adjacent cells by dragging the selection's fill handle (the small square in the bottom-right corner of the selected cell or range). Excel copies the original selection to the cells that you highlight while dragging. For more control over the AutoFill operation, click the AutoFill Options button that appears after you've released the mouse button, or drag the fill handle with the right mouse button. Each method shows a context menu with additional options, although not the same menu.

Copying a Range to Other Sheets

You can use the copy procedures described previously to copy a cell or range to another worksheet, even if the worksheet is in a different workbook. You must, of course, activate the other worksheet before you select the location to which you want to copy.

Excel offers a quicker way to copy a cell or range and paste it to other worksheets in the same workbook:

1. **Select the range to copy.**
2. **Press Ctrl and click the sheet tabs for the worksheets to which you want to copy the information.** Excel displays Group in the workbook's title bar.
3. **Choose Home ⇨ Editing ⇨ Fill ⇨ Across Worksheets.** A dialog box appears to ask you what you want to copy (All, Contents, or Formats).
4. **Make your choice and then click OK.** Excel copies the selected range to the selected worksheets; the new copy occupies the same cells in the selected worksheets as the original occupies in the initial worksheet.

CAUTION

Be careful with the Home ⟶ Editing ⟶ Fill ⟶ Across Worksheets command because Excel doesn't warn you when the destination cells contain information. You can quickly overwrite lots of cells with this command and not even realize it. So make sure that you check your work, and use Undo if the result isn't what you expected.

Using the Office Clipboard to Paste

Whenever you cut or copy information in an Office program such as Excel, you can place the data on both the Windows Clipboard and the Office Clipboard. When you copy information to the Office Clipboard, you append the information to the Office Clipboard instead of replacing what is already there. With multiple items stored on the Office Clipboard, you can then paste the items either individually or as a group.

To use the Office Clipboard, you first need to open it. Use the dialog box launcher on the bottom right of the Home ⇨ Clipboard group to toggle the Clipboard task pane on and off.

TIP

To make the Clipboard task pane open automatically, click the Options button near the bottom of the task pane and choose Show Office Clipboard Automatically.

After you open the Clipboard task pane, select the first cell or range that you want to copy to the Office Clipboard and copy it by using any of the preceding techniques. Repeat this process, selecting the next cell or range that you want to copy. As soon as you copy the information, the Office Clipboard task pane shows you the number of items that you've copied and a brief description (it will hold up to 24 items). Figure 7.9 shows the Office Clipboard with five copied items.

FIGURE 7.9

Use the Clipboard task pane to copy and paste multiple items.

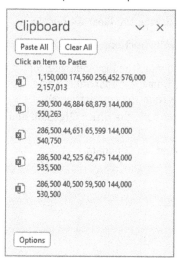

When you're ready to paste information, select the cell into which you want to paste it. To paste an individual item, click it in the Clipboard task pane. To paste all the items that you've copied, click the Paste All button (which is at the top of the Clipboard task pane). The items are pasted, one after the other.

The Paste All button is useful when you want to stack data from multiple columns into one. Figure 7.10 shows a rectangular range of data in the process of being converted to a single column. The ranges for Q2, Q3, and Q4 were copied to the clipboard separately. The Paste All button was used to paste the values starting below the Q1 total.

FIGURE 7.10

Use Paste All to convert multiple columns to one.

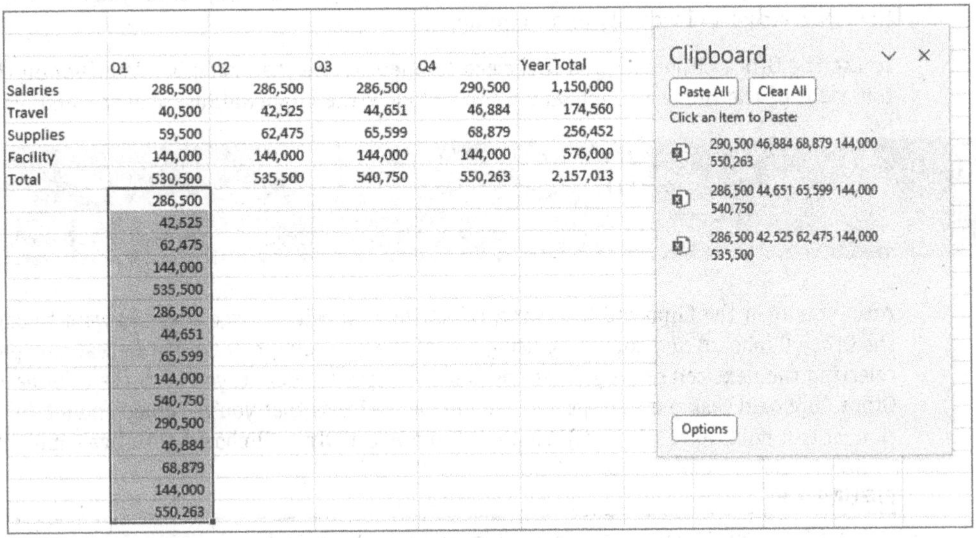

You can clear the contents of the Office Clipboard by clicking the Clear All button.

The following items about the Office Clipboard and how it functions are worth noting:

- Excel pastes the contents of the Windows Clipboard (the last item you copied to the Office Clipboard) when you paste by choosing Home ⇨ Clipboard ⇨ Paste, by pressing Ctrl+V, or by right-clicking and choosing Paste from the context menu.
- The last item that you cut or copied appears on both the Office Clipboard and the Windows Clipboard.
- Clearing the Office Clipboard also clears the Windows Clipboard.

> **CAUTION**
>
> The Office Clipboard has a serious problem that limits its usefulness for Excel users: If you copy a range that contains formulas, the formulas are not transferred when you paste from the Clipboard task pane to a different range. Only the values are pasted. Furthermore, Excel doesn't even warn you about this fact.

Pasting in Special Ways

You may not always want to copy everything from the source range to the destination range. For example, you may want to copy only the formula results rather than the formulas themselves. Or you may want to copy the number formats from one range to another without overwriting any existing data or formulas.

To control what is copied into the destination range, choose Home ➪ Clipboard ➪ Paste (bottom half with small down arrow) and use the drop-down menu shown in Figure 7.11. When you hover your mouse pointer over an icon, you'll see a preview of the pasted information in the destination range. Click the icon to use the selected paste option.

FIGURE 7.11

Excel offers several pasting options, with preview. Here, the information is copied from C4:C8 and is being pasted beginning at cell C14 using the Transpose option.

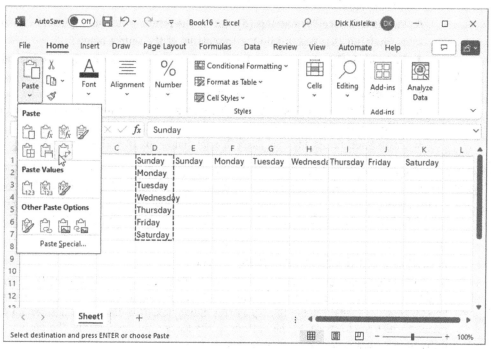

The paste options are as follows:

- **Paste (P):** Pastes the cell's contents, formula, formats, and data validation from the Windows Clipboard.
- **Formulas (F):** Pastes formulas but not formatting.
- **Formulas & Number Formatting (O):** Pastes formulas and number formatting only.
- **Keep Source Formatting (K):** Pastes formulas and all formatting.
- **No Borders (B):** Pastes everything except borders that appear in the source range.
- **Keep Source Column Widths (W):** Pastes formulas and duplicates the column width(s) of the copied cells.
- **Transpose (T).** Changes the orientation of the copied range. Rows become columns, and columns become rows. Any formulas in the copied range are adjusted so that they work properly when transposed.
- **Merge Conditional Formatting (G):** Displayed only when the copied cells contain conditional formatting. When clicked, it merges the copied conditional formatting with any conditional formatting in the destination range.
- **Values (V):** Pastes the results of formulas. The destination for the copy can be a new range or the original range. In the latter case, Excel replaces the original formulas with their current values.
- **Values & Number Formatting (A):** Pastes the results of formulas plus the number formatting.
- **Values & Source Formatting (E):** Pastes the results of formulas plus all formatting.
- **Formatting (R):** Pastes only the formatting of the source range.
- **Paste Link (N):** Creates formulas in the destination range that refer to the cells in the copied range.
- **Picture (U):** Pastes the copied information as a picture.
- **Linked Picture (I):** Pastes the copied information as a "live" picture that is updated if the source range is changed.
- **Paste Special:** Displays the Paste Special dialog box (described in the next section).

> **NOTE**
>
> After you paste, you're offered another chance to change your mind. A Paste Options button appears at the lower right of the pasted range. Click it (or press Ctrl), and you will see the Paste option icons again.

Using the Paste Special Dialog Box

For yet another pasting method, choose Home ⇨ Clipboard ⇨ Paste ⇨ Paste Special to display the Paste Special dialog box (see Figure 7.12). You can also right-click and choose Paste Special from the context menu to display this dialog box. This dialog box has several options, some of which are identical to the buttons in the Paste drop-down menu. The options that are different are explained in the following list:

FIGURE 7.12

The Paste Special dialog box

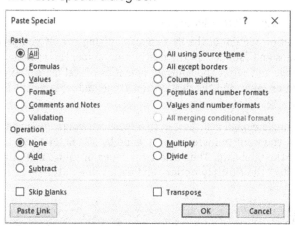

- **Comments And Notes:** Copies only the cell comments and cell notes from a cell or range. This option doesn't copy cell contents or formatting.
- **Validation:** Copies the validation criteria so that the same data validation will apply. Data validation is applied by choosing Data ⇨ Data Tools ⇨ Data Validation.
- **All Using Source Theme:** Pastes everything but uses the formatting from the document theme of the source. This option is relevant only if you're pasting information from a different workbook and the workbook uses a different document theme from the active workbook.
- **Column Widths:** Makes the column width of the destination range the same as the source range.
- **All Merging Conditional Formats:** Merges the copied conditional formatting with any conditional formatting in the destination range. This option is enabled only when you're copying a range that contains conditional formatting.

> **NOTE**
>
> Excel has several different Paste Special dialog boxes, each with different options. The one displayed depends on what's copied. This section describes the Paste Special dialog box that appears when a range or cell has been copied.

> **TIP**
>
> For the Paste Special command to be available, you need to copy a cell or range. (Choosing Home ⁖ Clipboard ⁖ Cut doesn't work.)

In addition, the Paste Special dialog box enables you to perform other operations, described in the following sections.

Performing Mathematical Operations Without Formulas

The option buttons in the Operation section of the Paste Special dialog box let you perform an arithmetic operation on values and formulas in the destination range. For example, you can copy a range to another range and select the Multiply operation. Excel multiplies the corresponding values in the source range and the destination range and replaces the destination range with the new values.

This feature also works with a single copied cell, pasted to a multicell range. Assume that you have a range of values, and you want to increase each value by 5%. Enter **105%** into any blank cell and copy that cell to the Clipboard. Then select the range of values and bring up the Paste Special dialog box. Select the Multiply option, and each value in the range is multiplied by 105%.

CAUTION

If the destination range contains formulas, the formulas are also modified. In many cases, this is not what you want.

Skipping Blanks When Pasting

The Skip Blanks option in the Paste Special dialog box prevents Excel from overwriting cell contents in your paste area with blank cells from the copied range. This option is useful if you're copying a range to another area but don't want the blank cells in the copied range to overwrite existing data.

Transposing a Range

The Transpose option in the Paste Special dialog box changes the orientation of the copied range. Rows become columns, and columns become rows. Any formulas in the copied range are adjusted so that they work properly when transposed. Note that you can use this option with the other options in the Paste Special dialog box. Figure 7.13 shows an example of a horizontal range (A3:F8) that was pasted to a different range (A11:F16) using the Values And Number Formats option and the Transpose option.

TIP

If you click the Paste Link button in the Paste Special dialog box, you create formulas that link to the source range. As a result, the destination range automatically reflects changes in the source range.

FIGURE 7.13

Transposing a range changes the orientation as the information is pasted into the worksheet.

	A	B	C	D	E	F	G
1	Budget Summary						
2							
3		Q1	Q2	Q3	Q4	Year Total	
4	Salaries	286,500	286,500	286,500	290,500	1,150,000	
5	Travel	40,500	42,525	44,651	46,884	174,560	
6	Supplies	59,500	62,475	65,599	68,879	256,452	
7	Facility	144,000	144,000	144,000	144,000	576,000	
8	Total	530,500	535,500	540,750	550,263	2,157,013	
9							
10							
11		Salaries	Travel	Supplies	Facility	Total	
12	Q1	286,500	40,500	59,500	144,000	530,500	
13	Q2	286,500	42,525	62,475	144,000	535,500	
14	Q3	286,500	44,651	65,599	144,000	540,750	
15	Q4	290,500	46,884	68,879	144,000	550,263	
16	Year Total	1,150,000	174,560	256,452	576,000	2,157,013	
17							

Using Names to Work with Ranges

Cell and range address syntax of column letters and row numbers becomes second nature pretty quickly as you work in Excel. However, when you're ready to design really robust and well-documented spreadsheets, you'll need to use *named ranges*. Excel's named range feature allows you to assign descriptive names to cells and ranges. For example, you can give a cell a name such as Interest_Rate, or you can name a range JulySales. Working with these names (rather than cell or range addresses) has several advantages:

- A meaningful range name (such as Total_Income) is much easier to remember than a cell address (such as AC21).
- Entering a name is less error prone than entering a cell or range address, and if you type a name incorrectly in a formula, Excel will display a #NAME? error.
- You can quickly move to areas of your worksheet either by using the Name box, located at the left side of the Formula bar (click the arrow to display a list of defined names) or by choosing Home ⇨ Editing ⇨ Find & Select ⇨ Go To (or pressing F5 or Ctrl+G) and specifying the range name.
- Creating formulas is easier. You can paste a cell or range name into a formula by using Formula AutoComplete.

 See Chapter 4, "Introducing Formulas and Functions," for information on Formula AutoComplete.

- Names make your formulas more understandable and easier to use. A formula such as =Income–Taxes is certainly more intuitive than =D20–D40.

Creating Range Names in Your Workbooks

Excel provides several methods that you can use to create range names. Before you begin, however, be aware of a few rules:

- Names can't contain spaces. You may want to use an underscore character to separate words (such as Annual_Total).
- You can use any combination of letters and numbers, but the name must begin with a letter, underscore, or backslash. A name can't begin with a number (such as 3rdQuarter) or look like a cell address (such as QTR3). If these are desirable names, though, you can precede the name with an underscore or a backslash, for example, _3rdQuarter and \QTR3.
- Symbols—except for underscores, backslashes, and periods—aren't allowed.
- Names are limited to 255 characters, but it's a good practice to keep names as short as possible yet still meaningful.

> **CAUTION**
>
> Excel also uses a few names internally for its own use. Although you can create names that override Excel's internal names, you should avoid doing so. To be on the safe side, avoid using the following for names: Print_Area, Print_Titles, Consolidate_Area, and Sheet_Title. To learn how to delete a range name or rename a range, see "Managing Names," later in this chapter.

Using the Name Box

The fastest way to create a name is to use the Name box (to the left of the Formula bar). Select the cell or range to name, click the Name box, and type the name. Press Enter to create the name. (You must press Enter to actually record the name; if you type a name and then click in the worksheet, Excel doesn't create the name.)

If you type an invalid name (such as May21, which happens to be a cell address, MAY21), Excel activates that address and doesn't warn you that the name is not valid. If the name you type includes an invalid character, Excel displays an error message. If a name already exists, you can't use the Name box to change the range to which that name refers. Attempting to do so simply selects the range.

The Name box has a drop-down list that shows all names in the workbook. To choose a named cell or range, click the arrow on the right side of the Name box and choose the name. The name appears in the Name box, and Excel selects the named cell or range in the worksheet.

Using the New Name Dialog Box

For more control over naming cells and ranges, use the New Name dialog box. Start by selecting the cell or range that you want to name. Then choose Formulas ➪ Defined Names ➪ Define Name. Excel displays the New Name dialog box, shown in Figure 7.14. Note that this is a resizable dialog box. Click and drag a border to change the dimensions.

FIGURE 7.14

Create names for cells or ranges by using the New Name dialog box.

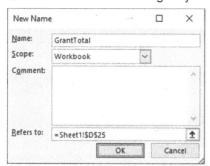

Type a name in the Name text field (or use the name that Excel proposes, if any). The selected cell or range address appears in the Refers To text field. Use the Scope drop-down list to indicate the scope for the name. The scope indicates where the name will be valid, and it's either the entire workbook or the worksheet in which the name is defined. If you like, you can add a comment that describes the named range or cell. Click OK to add the name to your workbook and close the dialog box.

Using the Create Names From Selection Dialog Box

You may have a worksheet that contains text that you want to use for names for adjacent cells or ranges. For example, you may want to use the text in column A to create names for the corresponding values in column B. Excel makes this task easy.

To create names by using adjacent text, start by selecting the name text and the cells that you want to name. (These items can be individual cells or ranges of cells.) The names must be adjacent to the cells that you're naming. (A multiple selection is allowed.) Then choose Formulas ⇨ Defined Names ⇨ Create From Selection. Excel displays the Create Names From Selection dialog box, shown in Figure 7.15.

The check marks in the Create Names From Selection dialog box are based on Excel's analysis of the selected range. For example, if Excel finds text in the first row of the selection, it proposes that you create names based on the top row. If Excel didn't guess correctly, you can change the check marks. Click OK, and Excel creates the names. Using the data in Figure 7.15, Excel creates the named ranges shown in the Name Manager in Figure 7.16.

NOTE

If the text contained in a cell would result in an invalid name, Excel modifies the name to make it valid. For example, if a cell contains the text Net Income (which is invalid for a name because it contains a space), Excel converts the space to an underscore character. If Excel encounters a value or a numeric formula where text should be, however, it doesn't convert it to a valid name. It simply doesn't create a name, and it does not inform you of that fact.

FIGURE 7.15

Use the Create Names From Selection dialog box to name cells using labels that appear in the worksheet.

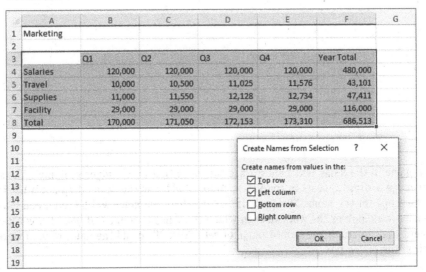

FIGURE 7.16

Use the Name Manager to work with range names.

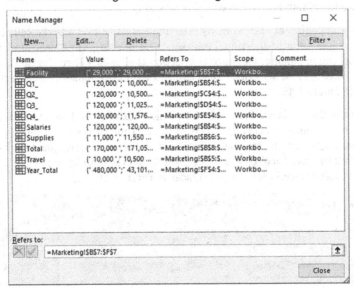

CAUTION

CAUTION

If the upper-left cell of the selection contains text and you choose the Top Row and Left Column options, Excel uses that text for the name of the entire range, excluding the top row and left column. So, after Excel creates the names, take a minute to make sure that they refer to the correct ranges. If Excel creates a name that is incorrect, you can delete or modify it by using the Name Manager (described next).

Managing Names

A workbook can have any number of named cells and ranges. If your workbook has many names, you should know about the Name Manager, which is shown in Figure 7.16.

The Name Manager appears when you choose Formulas ⇨ Defined Names ⇨ Name Manager (or press Ctrl+F3). The Name Manager has the following features:

- **Displays information about each name in the workbook:** You can resize the Name Manager dialog box, widen the columns to show more information, and even rearrange the order of the columns. You can also click a column heading to sort the information by the column.

- **Allows you to filter the displayed names:** Clicking the Filter button lets you show only those names that meet certain criteria. For example, you can view only the worksheet-level names.

- **Provides quick access to the New Name dialog box:** Click the New button to create a new name without closing the Name Manager.

- **Lets you edit names:** To edit a name, select it in the list, and then click the Edit button or double-click the name. You can change the name itself, modify the Refers To range, or edit the comment.

- **Lets you quickly delete unneeded names:** To delete a name, select it in the list and click Delete.

CAUTION

Be extra careful when deleting names. If the name is used in a formula, deleting the name causes the formula to become invalid. (It displays #NAME?.) It seems logical that Excel would replace the name with its actual address, but that doesn't happen. However, deleting a name can be undone, so if you find that formulas return #NAME? after you delete a name, choose Undo from the Quick Access Toolbar (or press Ctrl+Z) to get the name back.

If you delete the rows or columns that contain named cells or ranges, the names contain an invalid reference. For example, if cell A1 on Sheet1 is named Interest and you delete row 1 or column A, the name Interest then refers to =Sheet1!#REF! (an erroneous reference). If you use the name Interest in a formula, the formula displays #REF!.

TIP

To create a list of names in a worksheet, first select a cell in an empty area of your worksheet. The list is created at the active cell position and overwrites any information at that location. Press F3 to display the Paste Name dialog box, which lists all the defined names, and then click the Paste List button. Excel creates a list of all names in the workbook and their corresponding addresses.

Working with Tables

IN THIS CHAPTER

- Reviewing the parts of a table
- Adding a table to a worksheet
- Working with table data
- Changing how a table looks
- Working with table formulas

Tables provide a more structured way to organize, analyze, and format Excel data. This chapter discusses how to create a table, sort and filter table data, format a table, and work with table formulas.

Understanding a Table's Structure

A *table* is a specially designated area of a worksheet. When you designate a range as a table, Excel gives it special properties that make certain operations easier and that help prevent errors.

The purpose of a table is to enforce some structure around your data. If you're familiar with a table in a database (like Microsoft Access), then you already understand the concept of structured data. If not, don't worry. It's not difficult.

In a table, each row contains information about a single entity. In a table that holds employee information, each row will contain information about one employee (such as name, department, and hire date). Each column contains the same piece of information for each employee. The same column that holds the hire date for the first employee holds the hire date for all the other employees.

Figure 8.1 shows a simple table. The various components of a table are described in the following sections.

 This workbook, named `EmployeeTable.xlsx`, is available on this book's website at `www.wiley` `.com/go/excelquickandeasy`.

FIGURE 8.1

The areas that make up a table

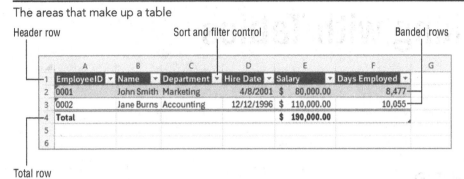

The Header Row

The *header row* is generally colored differently from the other rows. The names in the header identify the columns. If you have a formula that refers to a table, the header row will determine how the column is referred to. For example, the Days Employed column (column F) contains a formula that refers to the Hire Date column (column D). The formula is =NOW()-[@[Hire Date]]. If your table is longer than one screen, the header row will replace the normal column headers in Excel when you scroll down.

The header also contains *Filter buttons*. These drop-down buttons work exactly like Excel's normal AutoFilter feature. You can use them to sort and filter the table's data.

> **TIP**
> To display filter arrows in a contiguous range of cells that's not a table, first click a cell in the range. Then choose Data ⌐⸽ Filter to display the filter arrows.

The Data Body

The *data body* is one or more rows of data. By default, the rows are *banded*, that is, formatted with alternating colors. When you add new data to the table, the formatting of the existing data is applied to the new data. For example, if a column is formatted as Text, that column in the new row will also be formatted as Text. The same is true for conditional formatting.

It's not just formatting that applies to the new data. If a column contains a formula, that formula is automatically inserted into the new row. Data validation will also be transferred. You can make a robust data entry area knowing that the table structure will apply to new data.

One of the best features of tables is that as the data body expands, anything that refers to the table will expand automatically. If you were to base a PivotTable or a chart on your table, the PivotTable or chart would adjust as you added or deleted rows from the table.

The Total Row

The *total row* is not visible by default when you create a table. To show the total row, select the Total Row option in the Table Style Options group on the Table Design Ribbon. When you show the total row, the text *Total* is placed in the first column. You can change this to another value or to a formula.

Each cell in the total row has a drop-down arrow that you click to reveal a list of common functions. It's no accident that the list of functions resembles the arguments for the SUBTOTAL function. When you select a function from the list, Excel inserts a SUBTOTAL formula in the cell. The SUBTOTAL function ignores filtered cells, so the total will change if you filter the table.

In addition to the list of functions in the total row, there is a More Functions option at the bottom of the drop-down list. Selecting this option shows the Insert Function dialog box and makes all of Excel's functions available to you. Beyond that, you can simply type whatever formula you want in the total row.

The Resizing Handle

At the bottom right of the last cell in the table is the *resizing handle*. You can drag this handle to change the size of the table. Increasing the length of the table adds blank rows, copying down formatting, formulas, and data validation. Increasing the width of the table adds new columns with generic names like Column1, Column2, and so forth. You can change those names to something more meaningful.

Decreasing the size of the table simply changes what data is considered part of the table. It does not delete any data, formatting, formulas, or data validation. If you want to change what's in your table, you're better off deleting the columns and rows as you would any range rather than trying to do it with the resizing handle.

Creating a Table

Most of the time, you'll create a table from an existing range of data. However, Excel also allows you to create a table from an empty range so that you can fill in the data later. The following instructions assume that you already have a range of data that's suitable for a table:

1. **Make sure the range doesn't contain any completely blank rows or columns; otherwise, Excel will not guess the table range correctly.**

2. **Select any cell within the range.**

3. **Choose Insert ⇨ Tables ⇨ Table (or press Ctrl+T).** Excel responds with its Create Table dialog box, shown in Figure 8.2. Excel tries to guess the range, as well as whether the table has a header row. Most of the time, it guesses correctly. If not, make your corrections before you click OK.

8

FIGURE 8.2

Use the Create Table dialog box to verify that Excel guessed the table dimensions correctly.

	A	B	C	D	E	F	G	H	I	J
1	Agent	Date Listed	Area	List Price	Bedrooms	Baths	SqFt	Type	Pool	Sold
2	Adams	1/22/2025	Central	354,000	4	3.5	2,100	Condo	TRUE	TRUE
3	Adams	4/10/2025	Central	461,000	4	2	2,700	Condo	FALSE	FALSE
4	Adams	10/4/2025	Downtown	310,000	2	2.5	1,800	Split Level	FALSE	TRUE
5	Adams	1/19/2025	Downtown	325,000	2	3	1,900	Ranch	FALSE	TRUE
6	Adams	4/14/2025	Downtown	372,000	3	3.5	2,200	Split Level	FALSE	TRUE
7	Adams	3/17/2025	Downtown	374,000	4	3	2,200	Ranch	FALSE	TRUE
8	Adams	9/26/2025	Downtown	422,000	2					FALSE
9	Adams	1/10/2025	Downtown	446,000	2					TRUE
10	Adams	1/12/2025	Downtown	476,000	3					FALSE
11	Adams	9/22/2025	North	346,000	3					FALSE
12	Adams	4/15/2025	North	347,000	2					FALSE
13	Adams	9/12/2025	North	349,000	3					FALSE
14	Adams	5/21/2025	South	338,000	2					FALSE
15	Adams	4/16/2025	South	466,000	4	3	2,800	2 Story	FALSE	TRUE
16	Adams	11/22/2025	South	467,000	3	2	2,800	Ranch	TRUE	TRUE
17	Barnes	11/18/2025	Downtown	330,000	3	2	2,000	Ranch	TRUE	TRUE
18	Barnes	9/3/2025	Downtown	347,000	3	3	2,100	Split Level	TRUE	FALSE
19	Barnes	1/4/2025	Downtown	376,000	2	3	2,200	Ranch	FALSE	TRUE

Create Table dialog box overlay:

Create Table ? ×

Where is the data for your table?

$A$1:$J$80

☑ My table has headers

OK   Cancel

The range is converted to a table (using the default table style), and the Table Design tab of the Ribbon appears.

> **NOTE**
>
> Excel may not guess the table's dimensions correctly if the table isn't separated from other information by at least one empty row or column. If Excel guesses incorrectly, just specify the exact range for the table in the Create Table dialog box. Better yet, click Cancel and rearrange your worksheet such that the table is separated from your other data by at least one blank row and column.

To create a table from an empty range, select the range and choose Insert ⇨ Tables ⇨ Table. Excel creates the table, adds generic column headers (such as Column1 and Column2), and applies table formatting to the range. Almost always, you'll want to replace the generic column headers with more meaningful text.

Adding Data to a Table

If your table doesn't have a total row, the easiest way to enter data is simply to start typing in the row just below the table. When you enter something in a cell, Excel automatically expands the table and applies the formatting, formulas, and data validation to the new row. You can also paste a value in the next row. In fact, you could paste several rows' worth of data and the table will expand to accommodate.

If your table has a total row, you can't use that technique. In that case, you can insert rows into a table just as you would insert a row into any range. To insert a row, select a cell or the entire row and choose Home ⇨ Cells ⇨ Insert. When the selected range is inside a table, you'll see new entries on the Insert menu that deal with tables specifically. When you use these, the table is changed, but the data outside the table is unaffected.

When the selected cell is inside a table, the shortcut keys Ctrl − (minus sign) and Ctrl + (plus sign) work on the table only and not on data outside the table. Moreover, as opposed to when you're not in a table, those shortcuts work on the whole table row or column regardless of whether you've selected the whole row or column.

Sorting and Filtering Table Data

Each item in the header row of a table contains a drop-down arrow known as a *Filter button*. When clicked, the Filter button displays sorting and filtering options (see Figure 8.3).

FIGURE 8.3

Each column in a table has sorting and filtering options.

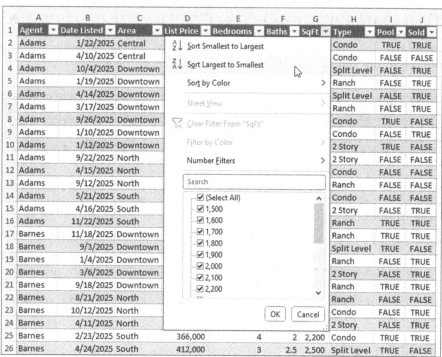

TIP

If you don't plan to sort or filter the data in a table, you can turn off the display of Filter buttons in a table's header row. Choose Table Design ➪ Table Style Options ➪ Filter Button to display or hide the drop-down arrows.

Sorting a Table

Sorting a table rearranges the rows based on the contents of a particular column. You may want to sort a table to put names in alphabetical order. Or maybe you want to sort your sales staff by the total sales made.

To sort a table by a particular column, click the Filter button in the column header and choose one of the sort commands. The exact command varies, depending on the type of data in the column.

You can also select Sort By Color to sort the rows based on the background or text color of the data. This option is relevant only if you've overridden the table style colors with custom formatting.

You can sort on any number of columns. The trick is to sort the least significant column first and then proceed until the most significant column is sorted last. For example, in the real estate table, you may want to sort the list by agent. And within each agent's group, sort the rows by area. Then within each area, sort the rows by list price in descending order. For this type of sort, first sort by the List Price column, then sort by the Area column, and then sort by the Agent column. Figure 8.4 shows the table sorted in this manner.

NOTE

When a column is sorted, the Filter button in the header row displays a different graphic to remind you that the table is sorted by that column.

Another way of performing a multiple-column sort is to use the Sort dialog box (choose Home ➪ Editing ➪ Sort & Filter ➪ Custom Sort). Or right-click any cell in the table and choose Sort ➪ Custom Sort from the context menu.

In the Sort dialog box, use the drop-down lists to specify the sort specifications. In this example, you start with Agent. Then click the Add Level button to insert another set of search controls. In this new set of controls, specify the sort specifications for the Area column. Then add another level and enter the specifications for the List Price column. Figure 8.5 shows the dialog box after entering the specifications for the three-column sort. This technique produces the same sort as described previously.

Filtering a Table

Filtering a table refers to displaying only the rows that meet certain conditions. (The other rows are hidden.)

FIGURE 8.4

A table after performing a three-column sort

	A	B	C	D	E	F	G	H	I	J
1	Agent	Date Listed	Area	List Price	Bedrooms	Baths	SqFt	Type	Pool	Sold
2	Adams	4/10/2025	Central	461,000	4	2	2,700	Condo	FALSE	FALSE
3	Adams	1/22/2025	Central	354,000	4	3.5	2,100	Condo	TRUE	TRUE
4	Adams	1/12/2025	Downtown	476,000	3	3	2,800	2 Story	TRUE	FALSE
5	Adams	1/10/2025	Downtown	446,000	2	2	2,700	Condo	FALSE	TRUE
6	Adams	9/26/2025	Downtown	422,000	2	3	2,500	Condo	TRUE	FALSE
7	Adams	3/17/2025	Downtown	374,000	4	3	2,200	Ranch	FALSE	TRUE
8	Adams	4/14/2025	Downtown	372,000	3	3.5	2,200	Split Level	FALSE	TRUE
9	Adams	1/19/2025	Downtown	325,000	2	3	1,900	Ranch	FALSE	TRUE
10	Adams	10/4/2025	Downtown	310,000	2	2.5	1,800	Split Level	FALSE	TRUE
11	Adams	9/12/2025	North	349,000	3	2	2,100	Ranch	FALSE	FALSE
12	Adams	4/15/2025	North	347,000	2	2	2,100	Condo	FALSE	FALSE
13	Adams	9/22/2025	North	346,000	3	2	2,100	2 Story	FALSE	FALSE
14	Adams	11/22/2025	South	467,000	3	2	2,800	Ranch	TRUE	TRUE
15	Adams	4/16/2025	South	466,000	4	3	2,800	2 Story	FALSE	TRUE
16	Adams	5/21/2025	South	338,000	2	3	2,000	Condo	FALSE	FALSE
17	Barnes	9/18/2025	Downtown	425,000	2	2	2,500	Ranch	TRUE	TRUE
18	Barnes	3/6/2025	Downtown	410,000	4	2	2,400	2 Story	FALSE	TRUE
19	Barnes	1/4/2025	Downtown	376,000	2	3	2,200	Ranch	FALSE	TRUE
20	Barnes	9/3/2025	Downtown	347,000	3	3	2,100	Split Level	TRUE	FALSE
21	Barnes	11/18/2025	Downtown	330,000	3	2	2,000	Ranch	TRUE	TRUE
22	Barnes	4/11/2025	North	467,000	3	2	2,800	2 Story	FALSE	TRUE
23	Barnes	10/12/2025	North	360,000	2	2.5	2,100	Condo	FALSE	TRUE

FIGURE 8.5

Using the Sort dialog box to specify a three-column sort

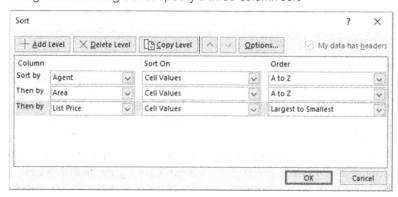

Note that entire worksheet rows are hidden. Therefore, if you have other data to the left or right of your table, that information may also be hidden when you filter the table. If you plan to filter your list, don't include any other data to the left or right of your table.

Using the real estate table, assume that you're interested only in the data for the Downtown area. Click the Filter button in the Area row header and deselect Select All, which deselects everything. Then place a check mark next to Downtown and click OK. The table, shown in Figure 8.6, is now filtered to display only the listings in the Downtown area. Notice that some of the row numbers are missing. These rows are hidden and contain data that does not meet the specified criteria.

FIGURE 8.6

This table is filtered to show the information for only one area.

	A	B	C	D	E	F	G	H	I	J
1	Agent	Date Listed	Area	List Price	Bedrooms	Baths	SqFt	Type	Pool	Sold
4	Adams	1/12/2025	Downtown	476,000	3	3	2,800	2 Story	TRUE	FALSE
5	Adams	1/10/2025	Downtown	446,000	2	2	2,700	Condo	FALSE	TRUE
6	Adams	9/26/2025	Downtown	422,000	2	3	2,500	Condo	TRUE	FALSE
7	Adams	3/17/2025	Downtown	374,000	4	3	2,200	Ranch	FALSE	TRUE
8	Adams	4/14/2025	Downtown	372,000	3	3.5	2,200	Split Level	TRUE	TRUE
9	Adams	1/19/2025	Downtown	325,000	2	3	1,900	Ranch	FALSE	TRUE
10	Adams	10/4/2025	Downtown	310,000	2	2.5	1,800	Split Level	FALSE	TRUE
17	Barnes	9/18/2025	Downtown	425,000	2	2	2,500	Ranch	TRUE	TRUE
18	Barnes	3/6/2025	Downtown	410,000	4	2	2,400	2 Story	FALSE	TRUE
19	Barnes	1/4/2025	Downtown	376,000	2	3	2,200	Ranch	FALSE	TRUE
20	Barnes	9/3/2025	Downtown	347,000	3	3	2,100	Split Level	TRUE	FALSE
21	Barnes	11/18/2025	Downtown	330,000	3	2	2,000	Ranch	TRUE	TRUE
30	Bennet	3/19/2025	Downtown	462,000	4	3.5	2,800	2 Story	TRUE	FALSE
31	Bennet	5/15/2025	Downtown	455,000	2	3	2,700	Condo	TRUE	FALSE
32	Bennet	7/8/2025	Downtown	412,000	3	2	2,500	2 Story	FALSE	FALSE
37	Chung	8/6/2025	Downtown	403,000	3	2	2,400	Split Level	TRUE	TRUE
41	Daily	1/20/2025	Downtown	479,000	4	3	2,900	Ranch	FALSE	TRUE
42	Daily	12/5/2025	Downtown	337,000	2	3	2,000	2 Story	TRUE	FALSE
45	Hamilton	2/2/2025	Downtown	536,000	4	2	3,200	Condo	TRUE	FALSE

Also notice that the Filter button in the Area column now shows a different graphic—an icon that indicates the column is filtered.

You can filter by multiple values in a column. For example, to filter the table to show only Downtown and Central, select both values in the drop-down list in the Area row header.

You can filter a table using any number of columns. For example, you may want to see only the Downtown listings in which Type is Condo. Just repeat the operation using the Type column. The table then displays only the rows in which Area is Downtown and Type is Condo.

For additional filtering options, select Text Filters (or Number Filters, if the column contains values). The options are fairly self-explanatory, and you have a great deal of flexibility in displaying only the rows in which you're interested. For example, you can display rows in which the List Price is greater than or equal to $300,000 and less than $400,000 (see Figure 8.7).

Also, you can right-click a cell and use the Filter command on the context menu. This menu item leads to several additional filtering options that enable you to filter data based on the contents of the selected cell or by formatting.

FIGURE 8.7

Specifying a more complex numeric filter

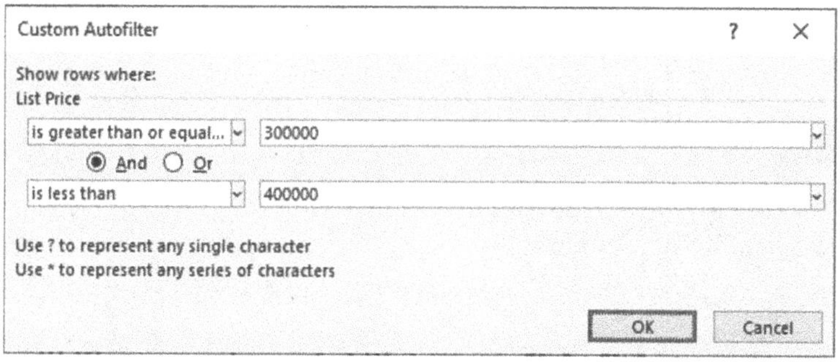

> **NOTE**
>
> As you may expect, when you use filtering, the total row is updated to show the total only for the visible rows.

When you copy data from a filtered table, only the visible data is copied. In other words, rows that are hidden by filtering aren't copied. This filtering makes it easy to copy a subset of a larger table and paste it to another area of your worksheet. Keep in mind, though, that the pasted data is not a table—it's just a normal range. You can, however, convert the copied range to a table.

To remove filtering for a column, open the drop-down in the row header and select Clear Filter. If you've filtered using multiple columns, it may be faster to remove all filters by choosing Data ➪ Sort & Filter ➪ Clear.

Filtering a Table with Slicers

Another way to filter a table is to use one or more *slicers*. This method is less flexible but more visually appealing. Slicers are particularly useful when the table will be viewed by novices or those who find the normal filtering techniques too complicated. Slicers are very visual, and it's easy to see exactly what type of filtering is in effect. A disadvantage of slicers is that they take up a lot of room on the screen.

To add one or more slicers, activate any cell in the table and choose Table Design ➪ Tools ➪ Insert Slicer. Excel responds with a dialog box that displays each header in the table (see Figure 8.8).

Place a check mark next to the field(s) that you want to filter. You can create a slicer for each column, but that's rarely needed. In most cases, you'll want to be able to filter the table by only a few fields. Click OK, and Excel creates a slicer for each field you specified.

FIGURE 8.8

Use the Insert Slicers dialog box to specify which slicers to create.

A slicer contains a button for every unique item in the field. In the real estate listing example, the slicer for the Agent field contains 14 buttons because the table has records for 14 different agents.

> **NOTE**
>
> Slicers may not be appropriate for columns that contain numeric data. For example, the real estate listing table has 78 different values in the List Price column. Therefore, a slicer for this column would have 78 buttons (and there's no way to group the values into numeric ranges). This is an example of how a slicer is not as flexible as normal filtering using Filter buttons.

To use a slicer, just click one of the buttons. The table displays only the rows that have a value that corresponds to the button. You can also press Ctrl to select multiple buttons and press Shift to select a continuous group of buttons, which would be useful for selecting a range of List Price values. The slicer also has a multiselect button at the top. Click that button to toggle multiselect mode, and you won't have to hold down the Ctrl key.

If your table has more than one slicer, it's filtered by the selected buttons in each slicer. To remove filtering for a particular slicer, click the Clear Filter icon in the upper-right corner of the slicer.

Use the tools in the Slicer Ribbon to change the appearance or layout of a slicer. You have quite a bit of flexibility.

Figure 8.9 shows a table with two slicers. The table is filtered to show only the records for Adams, Barnes, and Chung in the Downtown area.

FIGURE 8.9

The table is filtered by two slicers.

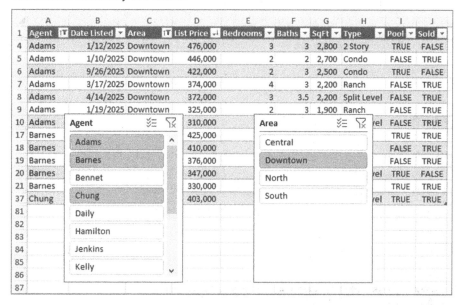

Changing the Table's Appearance

When you create a table, Excel applies the default table style. The actual appearance depends on which document theme is used in the workbook (see Chapter 9, "Formatting Worksheets"). If you prefer a different look, you can easily apply a different table style.

Select any cell in the table and choose Table Design ⇨ Table Styles. The Ribbon shows one row of styles, but if you click the More button at the bottom of the scrollbar to the right, Excel displays the Table Styles gallery, as shown in Figure 8.10. The styles are grouped into three categories: Light, Medium, and Dark. Notice that you get a "live" preview as you move your mouse among the styles. When you see one you like, just click to make it permanent. And yes, some are really ugly and practically illegible.

FIGURE 8.10

Excel offers many different table styles.

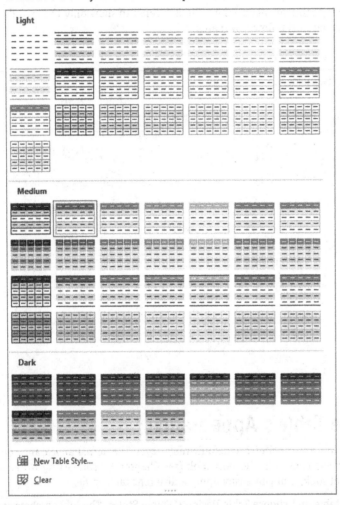

For a different set of color choices, choose Page Layout ⇨ Themes ⇨ Themes to select a different document theme.

For more information about themes, see Chapter 9.

You can change some elements of the style by using the options in the Table Design ⇨ Table Style Options group. These controls determine whether various elements of the table are displayed and whether some formatting options are in effect:

- **Header Row:** Toggles the display of the header row.
- **Total Row:** Toggles the display of the total row.
- **First Column:** Toggles special formatting for the first column. Depending on the table style used, this command might have no effect.
- **Last Column:** Toggles special formatting for the last column. Depending on the table style used, this command might have no effect.
- **Banded Rows:** Toggles the display of banded (alternating color) rows.
- **Banded Columns:** Toggles the display of banded columns.
- **Filter Button:** Toggles the display of the drop-down buttons in the table's header row.

> **TIP**
>
> If applying table styles isn't working, it's probably because the range was already formatted before you converted it to a table. Table formatting doesn't override normal formatting. To clear existing background fill colors, select the entire table and choose Home ⇨ Font ⇨ Fill Color ⇨ No Fill. To clear existing font colors, choose Home ⇨ Font ⇨ Font Color ⇨ Automatic. To clear existing borders, choose Home ⇨ Font ⇨ Borders ⇨ No Border. After you issue these commands, the table styles should work as expected.

8

If you'd like to create a custom table style, choose Table Design ⇨ Table Styles ⇨ New Table Style to display the New Table Style dialog box, shown in Figure 8.11. You can customize any or all of the 12 table elements. Select an element from the list, click Format, and specify the formatting for that element. When you're finished, give the new style a name and click OK. Your custom table style will appear in the Table Styles gallery in the Custom category.

Custom table styles are available only in the workbook in which they were created. However, if you copy a table that uses a custom style to a different workbook, the custom style will be available in the other workbook.

> **TIP**
>
> If you want to make changes to an existing table style, locate it in the Ribbon and right-click and then choose Duplicate from the context menu. Excel displays the Modify Table Style dialog box with all of the settings from the specified table style. Make your changes, give the style a new name, and click OK to save it as a custom table style.

FIGURE 8.11

Use this dialog box to create a new table style.

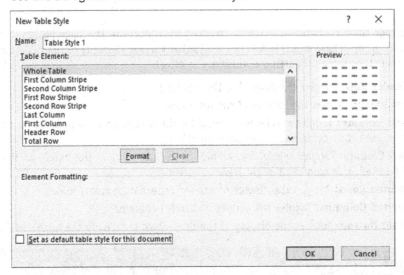

Using Formulas in Tables

As noted earlier in the chapter, a table may include a total row that's not visible by default. You can add and work with the total row to perform various calculations and turn it on and off as needed. In this section, we describe how total row formulas work with tables.

Summarizing Data in a Table

Figure 8.12 shows a simple table with three columns. We entered the data and then converted the range to a table by choosing Insert ⇨ Tables ⇨ Table. Note that we didn't define any names, but the table is named `Table1` by default.

 This workbook is available on this book's website at www.wiley.com/go/excelquickandeasy. It is named `table formulas.xlsx`.

If you'd like to calculate the total projected and total actual sales, you don't even need to write a formula. Simply click a button to add a row of summary formulas to the table:

1. **Activate any cell in the table.**

2. **Choose Table Design ⇨ Table Style Options and select Total Row.** Excel adds a total row to the table and displays the sum of each numeric column.

3. **To change the type of summary formula, activate a cell in the total row and use the drop-down list to change the type of summary formula to use** (see

Figure 8.13). For example, to calculate the average of the Actual column, select AVERAGE from the drop-down list in cell D15. Excel creates this formula:

```
=SUBTOTAL(101, [Actual])
```

FIGURE 8.12

A simple table with three columns of information

	A	B	C	D
1				
2		Month	Projected	Actual
3		Jan	4,000	3,255
4		Feb	4,000	4,102
5		Mar	4,000	3,982
6		Apr	5,000	4,598
7		May	5,000	5,873
8		Jun	5,000	4,783
9		Jul	5,000	5,109
10		Aug	6,000	5,982
11		Sep	6,000	6,201
12		Oct	7,000	6,833
13		Nov	8,000	7,983
14		Dec	9,000	9,821

FIGURE 8.13

A drop-down list enables you to select a summary formula for a table column.

Month	Projected	Actual
Jan	4,000	3,255
Feb	4,000	4,102
Mar	4,000	3,982
Apr	5,000	4,598
May	5,000	5,873
Jun	5,000	4,783
Jul	5,000	5,109
Aug	6,000	5,982
Sep	6,000	6,201
Oct	7,000	6,833
Nov	8,000	7,983
Dec	9,000	9,821
Total	68,000	68,522

None
Average
Count
Count Numbers
Max
Min
Sum
StdDev
Var
More Functions...

For the SUBTOTAL function, 101 is an enumerated argument that represents AVERAGE. The second argument for the SUBTOTAL function is the column name in square brackets. Using the column name within brackets creates "structured" references within a table. (We discuss this further in the upcoming section "Referencing Data in a Table.")

> **NOTE**
> You can toggle the total row display via Table Design ⇨ Table Style Options ⇨ Total Row. If you turn it off, the summary options you selected will be displayed again when you turn it back on.

Using Formulas Within a Table

In many cases, you'll want to use formulas within a table to perform calculations that use other columns in the table. For example, in the table shown in Figure 8.14, you may want a column that shows the difference between the Actual and Projected amounts. To add this formula, follow these steps:

1. **Activate cell E2 and type Difference for the column header.** After you press Enter, Excel automatically expands the table for you to include the new column.

2. **Move to cell E3 and type an equals sign to signify the beginning of a formula.**

3. **Press the Left Arrow key.** Excel displays [@Actual], which is the column heading, in the Formula bar.

4. **Type a minus sign and then press the Left Arrow key twice.** Excel displays [@Projected] in your formula.

5. **Press Enter to end the formula.** Excel copies the formula to all rows in the table.

Figure 8.14 shows the table with the new column.

FIGURE 8.14

The Difference column contains a formula.

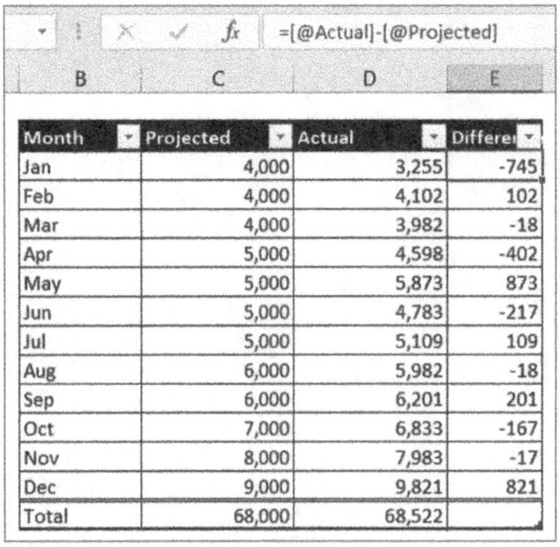

Month	Projected	Actual	Difference
Jan	4,000	3,255	-745
Feb	4,000	4,102	102
Mar	4,000	3,982	-18
Apr	5,000	4,598	-402
May	5,000	5,873	873
Jun	5,000	4,783	-217
Jul	5,000	5,109	109
Aug	6,000	5,982	-18
Sep	6,000	6,201	201
Oct	7,000	6,833	-167
Nov	8,000	7,983	-17
Dec	9,000	9,821	821
Total	68,000	68,522	

Examine the table, and you will find this formula for all cells in the Difference column:

```
=[@Actual]-[@Projected]
```

Although the formula was entered into the first row of the table, that's not necessary. Any time a formula is entered into an empty table column, it will automatically fill all of the cells in that column. If you need to edit the formula, Excel will automatically copy the edited formula to the other cells in the column.

NOTE

The at symbol (@) that precedes the column header represents "this row." So `[@Actual]` means "the value in the Actual column in this row."

These steps use the pointing technique to create the formula. Alternatively, you could have entered the formula manually using standard cell references rather than column headers. For example, you could have entered the following formula in cell E3:

```
=D3-C3
```

If you type the cell references, Excel will still copy the formula to the other cells automatically.

One thing should be clear, however, about formulas that use the column headers instead of cell references—they're much easier to understand.

TIP

To override the automatic column formulas, access the Proofing tab of the Excel Options dialog box. Click AutoCorrect Options and then select the AutoFormat As You Type tab in the AutoCorrect dialog box. Deselect the option Fill Formulas In Tables To Create Calculated Columns.

Referencing Data in a Table

Excel offers some other ways to refer to data that's contained in a table by using the table name and column headers.

You can, of course, use standard cell references to refer to data in a table, but using the table name and column headers has a distinct advantage: The names adjust automatically if the table size changes by inserting or deleting rows. In addition, formulas that use table names and column headers will adjust automatically if you change the name of the table or give a new name to a column.

To refer to the Table1 table shown in the figures for this section, you can use the table name. For instance, to calculate the sum of all the data in the table, enter this formula into a cell outside the table:

```
=SUM(Table1)
```

This formula will return the sum of all the data (excluding calculated total row values, if any), even if rows or columns are added or deleted. And if you change the name of `Table1`, Excel will adjust formulas that refer to that table automatically. For example, if you renamed `Table1` to `AnnualData`, the preceding formula would change to:

```
=SUM(AnnualData)
```

Most of the time, a formula will refer to a specific column in the table. The following formula returns the sum of the data in the Actual column:

```
=SUM(Table1[Actual])
```

Notice that the column name is enclosed in square brackets. Again, the formula adjusts automatically if you change the text in the column heading.

Even better, Excel provides some helpful assistance when you create a formula that refers to data within a table. Figure 8.15 shows the formula AutoComplete feature helping to create a formula by showing a list of the elements in the table. Notice that, in addition to the column headers in the table, Excel lists other table elements that you can reference: `#All`, `#Data`, `#Headers`, `#Totals`, and `@ - This Row`.

FIGURE 8.15

The formula AutoComplete feature is useful when creating a formula that refers to data in a table.

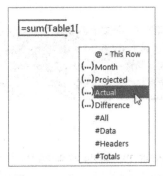

Formatting Worksheets

IN THIS CHAPTER

- Understanding how formatting can improve your worksheets
- Getting to know the formatting tools
- Using formatting in your worksheets
- Using named styles for easier formatting
- Understanding document themes

Formatting your worksheet is more than just making your worksheet pretty. Proper formatting can help users understand the purpose of the worksheet and help prevent data entry errors.

Stylistic formatting isn't essential for every workbook that you develop, especially if it's only for your own use. On the other hand, it takes only a few moments to apply some simple formatting, and after you apply it, the formatting will remain in place without further effort on your part.

Getting to Know the Formatting Tools

Figure 9.1 shows how even simple formatting can significantly improve a worksheet's readability. The unformatted worksheet (on the left) is perfectly functional but not very readable compared to the formatted worksheet (on the right).

 This workbook is available on this book's website at www.wiley.com/go/excelquickandeasy. **The file is named** loan payments.xlsx.

The Excel cell formatting tools are available in three locations:

- On the Home tab of the Ribbon
- On the Mini toolbar that appears when you right-click a selected range or a cell
- From the Format Cells dialog box

In addition, many common formatting commands have keyboard shortcuts.

FIGURE 9.1

Simple formatting can greatly improve the appearance of your worksheet.

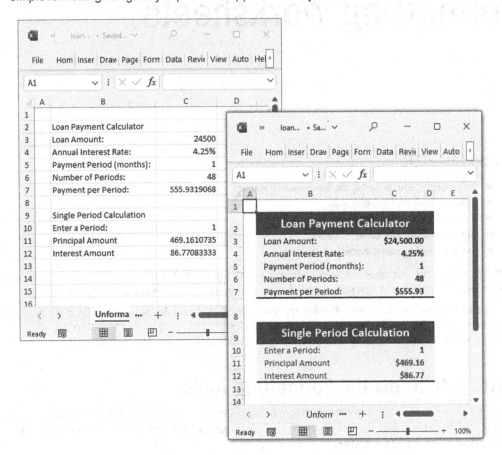

Using the Formatting Tools on the Home Tab

The Home tab of the Ribbon provides quick access to the most commonly used formatting options. Start by selecting the cell or range you want to format. Then use the appropriate tool in the Font, Alignment, or Number group.

Using these tools is intuitive, and the best way to familiarize yourself with them is to experiment. Enter some data, select some cells, and then click the controls to change the appearance. Note that some of these controls are actually drop-down lists. Click the small arrow on the button, and the button expands to display more choices.

Using the Mini Toolbar

When you right-click a cell or a range selection, you get a context menu. In addition, the Mini toolbar appears above or below the context menu. Figure 9.2 shows how this toolbar looks. The Mini toolbar for cell formatting contains the most commonly used controls from the Home tab of the Ribbon.

FIGURE 9.2

The Mini toolbar appears above or below the right-click context menu.

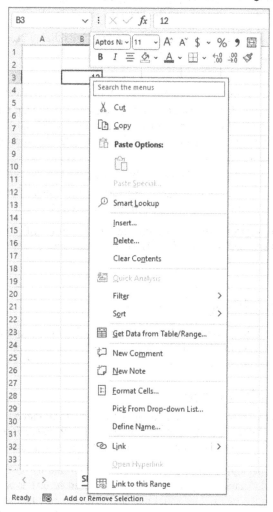

If you use a tool on the Mini toolbar, the context menu disappears, but the toolbar remains visible so that you can apply other formatting to the selected cells. To hide the Mini toolbar, just click in any cell or press Esc.

Using the Format Cells Dialog Box

The formatting controls available on the Home tab of the Ribbon are sufficient most of the time, but some types of formatting require that you use the Format Cells dialog box. This tabbed dialog box lets you apply nearly any type of stylistic formatting and number formatting. The formats that you choose in the Format Cells dialog box apply to the selected cells. Later sections in this chapter cover some of the tabs of the Format Cells dialog box.

After selecting the cell or range to format, you can display the Format Cells dialog box by using any of the following methods:

- Press Ctrl+1.
- Click the dialog box launcher in Home ➪ Font, Home ➪ Alignment, or Home ➪ Number. (The dialog box launcher is the small downward-pointing arrow icon displayed to the right of the group name in the Ribbon.) When you display the Format Cells dialog box using a dialog box launcher, the dialog box is displayed with the appropriate tab visible.
- Right-click the selected cell or range and choose Format Cells from the context menu.
- Click the More command in some of the drop-down controls in the Ribbon. For example, the Home ➪ Font ➪ Border drop-down includes an item named More Borders.

The Format Cells dialog box contains six tabs: Number, Alignment, Font, Border, Fill, and Protection. The following sections contain more information about the formatting options available in this dialog box.

Formatting Your Worksheet

Excel offers most of the same formatting options as other Office applications like Word or PowerPoint. As you might expect, cell-related formatting like fill color and borders feature more prominently in Excel than in some of the other applications.

Using Fonts to Format Your Worksheet

You can use different fonts, font sizes, or text attributes in your worksheets to make various parts stand out, such as the headers for a table. You also can adjust the font size. For example, using a smaller font allows for more information to appear on a single screen or printed page.

By default, Excel uses the 11-point (pt) Aptos Narrow font. A font is described by its typeface (Aptos Narrow, Calibri, Cambria, Arial, Times New Roman, Courier New, and so on) as well as by its size, measured in points. (Seventy-two points equal one inch.) Excel's row height, by default, is 15 pt. Therefore, 11-pt type entered into 15-pt rows leaves a small amount of blank space between the characters in vertically adjacent rows.

> **TIP**
>
> If you haven't manually changed a row's height, Excel automatically adjusts the row height based on the tallest text that you enter into the row.

> **TIP**
>
> If you plan to distribute a workbook to other users, remember that Excel does not embed fonts. Therefore, you should stick with the standard fonts that are included with Windows or Microsoft Office. If you open a workbook and your system doesn't have the font used in the workbook, Windows attempts to use a similar font. Sometimes this attempt works; other times it doesn't.

Use the Font and Font Size tools in the Font group on the Home tab of the Ribbon (or on the Mini toolbar) to change the font or size for selected cells.

You also can use the Font tab in the Format Cells dialog box to choose fonts, as shown in Figure 9.3. This tab enables you to control several other font attributes that aren't available elsewhere. Besides choosing the font and font size, you can change the font style (bold, italic), underlining, color, and effects (strikethrough, superscript, or subscript). If you select the Normal Font check box, Excel displays the selections for the font defined for the Normal style. We discuss styles later in this chapter (see "Using Named Styles for Easier Formatting").

FIGURE 9.3

The Font tab of the Format Cells dialog box gives you many additional font attribute options.

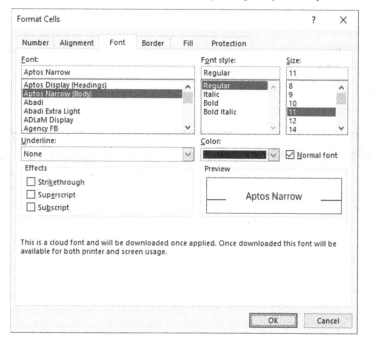

This is a cloud font and will be downloaded once applied. Once downloaded this font will be available for both printer and screen usage.

Figure 9.4 shows several examples of font formatting. In this figure, gridlines were turned off to make the underlining more visible. Notice, in the figure, that Excel provides four different underlining styles. In the two nonaccounting underline styles, only the cell contents are underlined. In the two accounting underline styles, the entire width of the cells is always underlined.

FIGURE 9.4

You can choose many different font formatting options for your worksheets.

If you prefer to keep both hands on the keyboard, you can use the following shortcut keys to format a selected range quickly:

- **Ctrl+B:** Bold
- **Ctrl+I:** Italic
- **Ctrl+U:** Underline
- **Ctrl+5:** Strikethrough

These shortcut keys act as a toggle. For example, you can turn bold on and off by repeatedly pressing Ctrl+B.

Using Multiple Formatting Styles in a Single Cell

If a cell contains text (as opposed to a value or a formula), you can apply formatting to individual characters in the cell. To do so, switch to Edit mode (press F2, or double-click the cell) and then select the characters that you want to format. You can select characters either by dragging the mouse over them or by pressing the Shift key as you press the left or right arrow key.

This technique is useful if you need to apply superscript or subscript formatting to a few characters in the cell (refer to Figure 9.4 for examples).

After you select the characters to format, use any of the standard formatting techniques, including options in the Format Cells dialog box. To display the Format Cells dialog box when editing a cell, press Ctrl+1. The changes apply only to the selected characters in the cell. This technique doesn't work with cells that contain values or formulas.

TIP

The Number tab of the Format Cells dialog box enables you to apply the desired formatting to cells containing numeric entries. For example, you can specify whether or not a numeric entry includes the 1000 separator (a comma in the US), a currency symbol, the number of decimal places, and parentheses or a red font color for a negative value. The Category List at the left side of the tab enables you to select and customize predefined formats for Number, Currency, Accounting, Date, Time, and Percentage values, and more. You also can apply some number formatting using the controls in the Number group of the Home tab.

Changing Text Alignment

The contents of a cell can be aligned horizontally and vertically. By default, Excel aligns numbers to the right and text to the left. All cells use bottom alignment by default.

Overriding these defaults is a simple matter. The most commonly used alignment commands are in the Alignment group on the Home tab of the Ribbon. Use the Alignment tab of the Format Cells dialog box for even more options (see Figure 9.5).

Choosing Horizontal Alignment Options

Horizontal alignment options, which control how cell contents are distributed across the width of the cell (or cells), are available from the Format Cells dialog box:

- **General:** Aligns numbers to the right, aligns text to the left, and centers logical and error values. This option is the default horizontal alignment.
- **Left:** Aligns the cell contents to the left side of the cell. If the text is wider than the cell, the text spills over to the cell on the right. If the cell on the right isn't empty, the text is truncated and not completely visible. This option is also available on the Ribbon.
- **Center:** Centers the cell contents in the cell. If the text is wider than the cell, the text spills over to cells on either side if they're empty. If the adjacent cells aren't empty, the text is truncated and not completely visible. This option is also available on the Ribbon.
- **Right:** Aligns the cell contents to the right side of the cell. If the text is wider than the cell, the text spills over to the cell on the left. If the cell on the left isn't empty, the text is truncated and not completely visible. This option is also available on the Ribbon.

9

- **Fill:** Repeats the contents of the cell until the cell's width is filled. If cells to the right also are formatted with Fill alignment, they also are filled.
- **Justify:** Justifies the text to the left and right of the cell. This option is applicable only if the cell is formatted as wrapped text and uses more than one line.
- **Center Across Selection:** Centers the text over the selected columns. This option is useful for centering a heading over several columns.
- **Distributed:** Distributes the text evenly across the cell, adding additional whitespace between words where necessary.

FIGURE 9.5

The full range of alignment options is available on the Alignment tab of the Format Cells dialog box.

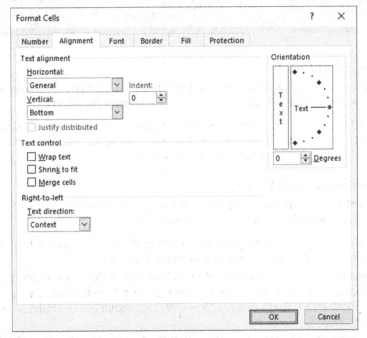

> **NOTE**
>
> If you choose Left, Right, or Distributed, you can also adjust the Indent setting, which adds horizontal space between the cell border and the text.

Figure 9.6 shows examples of text that uses three types of horizontal alignment: Left, Justify, and Distributed (with an indent).

FIGURE 9.6

The same text, displayed with three types of horizontal alignment

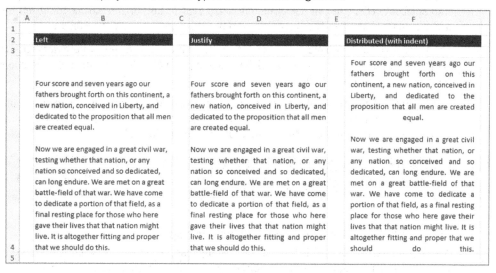

 If you want to experiment with text alignment settings, this workbook is available at this book's website at www.wiley.com/go/excelquickandeasy. **The file is named** text alignment.xlsx.

Choosing Vertical Alignment Options

Vertical alignment options typically aren't used as often as horizontal alignment options. In fact, these settings are useful only if you've adjusted row heights so that they're considerably taller than normal.

Here are the vertical alignment options available in the Format Cells dialog box:

- **Top:** Aligns the cell contents to the top of the cell. This option is also available on the Ribbon.
- **Center:** Centers the cell contents vertically in the cell. This option is also available on the Ribbon.
- **Bottom:** Aligns the cell contents to the bottom of the cell. This option is also available on the Ribbon and is the default vertical alignment.
- **Justify:** Justifies the text vertically in the cell; this option is applicable only if the cell is formatted as wrapped text and uses more than one line. This setting can be used to increase the line spacing.
- **Distributed:** Distributes the text evenly between the top and bottom of the cell, adding additional whitespace between lines where necessary. If there is only one line of text in the cell, it's identical to the Center option.

Wrapping or Shrinking Text to Fit the Cell

If you have text too wide to fit the column width but you don't want that text to spill over into adjacent cells, you can use either the Wrap Text option or the Shrink To Fit option to accommodate that text. The Wrap Text option is also available on the Ribbon.

The Wrap Text option displays the text on multiple lines in the cell, if necessary. Use this option to display lengthy headings without having to make the columns too wide and without reducing the size of the text.

The Shrink To Fit option reduces the size of the text so that it fits into the cell without spilling over to the next cell. The times that this command is useful seem to be rare. Unless the text is just slightly too long, the result is almost always illegible.

NOTE

If you apply Wrap Text formatting to a cell, you can't use the Shrink To Fit formatting.

Merging Worksheet Cells to Create Additional Text Space

Another formatting option is the ability to merge two or more cells. When you merge cells, you don't combine the contents of cells. Rather, you combine a group of cells into a single cell that occupies the same space. The worksheet shown in Figure 9.7 contains four sets of merged cells. Range C2:I2 has been merged into a single cell and so have ranges J2:P2, B4:B8, and B9:B13. In the latter two cases, the text orientation has also been changed (see "Displaying Text at an Angle," later in this chapter).

FIGURE 9.7

Merge worksheet cells to make them act as if they were a single cell.

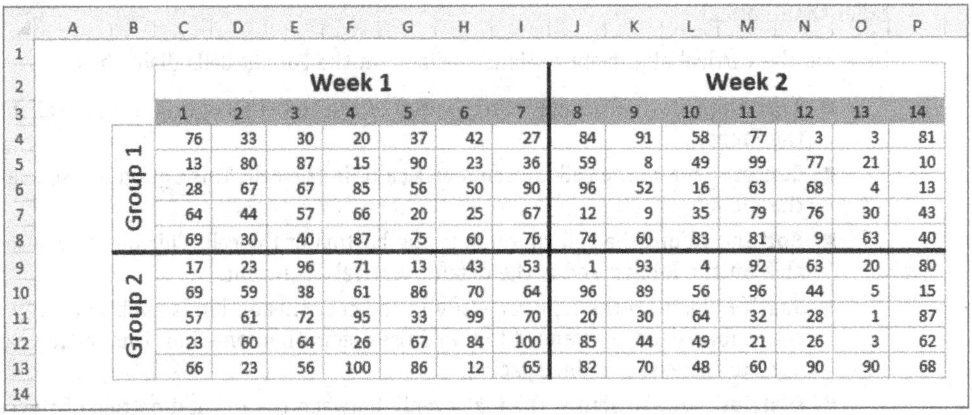

				Week 1						Week 2				
		1	2	3	4	5	6	7	8	9	10	11	12	13	14
		76	33	30	20	37	42	27	84	91	58	77	3	3	81
		13	80	87	15	90	23	36	59	8	49	99	77	21	10
	Group 1	28	67	67	85	56	50	90	96	52	16	63	68	4	13
		64	44	57	66	20	25	67	12	9	35	79	76	30	43
		69	30	40	87	75	60	76	74	60	83	81	9	63	40
		17	23	96	71	13	43	53	1	93	4	92	63	20	80
		69	59	38	61	86	70	64	96	89	56	96	44	5	15
	Group 2	57	61	72	95	33	99	70	20	30	64	32	28	1	87
		23	60	64	26	67	84	100	85	44	49	21	26	3	62
		66	23	56	100	86	12	65	82	70	48	60	90	90	68

You can merge any number of cells occupying any number of rows and columns. In fact, you can merge all 17 billion cells in a worksheet into a single cell—although there probably isn't a good reason to do so, except maybe to play a trick on a coworker.

The range that you intend to merge should be empty, except for the upper-left cell. If any of the other cells that you intend to merge are not empty, Excel displays a warning. If you continue, all the data (except in the upper-left cell) will be deleted.

You can use the Alignment tab of the Format Cells dialog box to merge cells, but using the Merge & Center control in the Alignment group on the Ribbon (or on the Mini toolbar) is simpler. To merge cells, select the cells that you want to merge and then click the Merge & Center button. The cells will be merged, and the content in the upper-left cells will be centered horizontally. The Merge & Center button acts as a toggle. To unmerge cells, select the merged cells and click the Merge & Center button again.

After you merge cells, you can change the alignment to something other than Center by using the controls in the Home ⇨ Alignment group.

The Home ⇨ Alignment ⇨ Merge & Center control contains a drop-down list with these additional options:

- **Merge Across:** When a multirow range is selected, this command creates multiple merged cells—one for each row.
- **Merge Cells:** Merges the selected cells without applying the Center attribute.
- **Unmerge Cells:** Unmerges the selected cells.

Displaying Text at an Angle

In some cases, you may want to create more visual impact by displaying text at an angle within a cell. You can display text horizontally, vertically, or at any angle between 90 degrees up and 90 degrees down.

From the Home ⇨ Alignment ⇨ Orientation drop-down list, you can apply the most common text angles. For more control, use the Alignment tab of the Format Cells dialog box. In the Format Cells dialog box (refer to Figure 9.5), use the Degrees spinner control—or just drag the red pointer in the gauge. You can specify a text angle between –90 and +90 degrees.

Figure 9.8 shows an example of text displayed at a 45-degree angle.

NOTE

Rotated text may look a bit distorted onscreen, but the printed output is usually of much better quality.

Using Colors and Shading

Excel provides the tools to create some colorful worksheets. You can change the color of the text or add colors to the backgrounds of the worksheet cells. Early versions of Excel had a limited palette of 56 colors, but modern versions have more than 16 million.

FIGURE 9.8

Rotate text for additional visual impact.

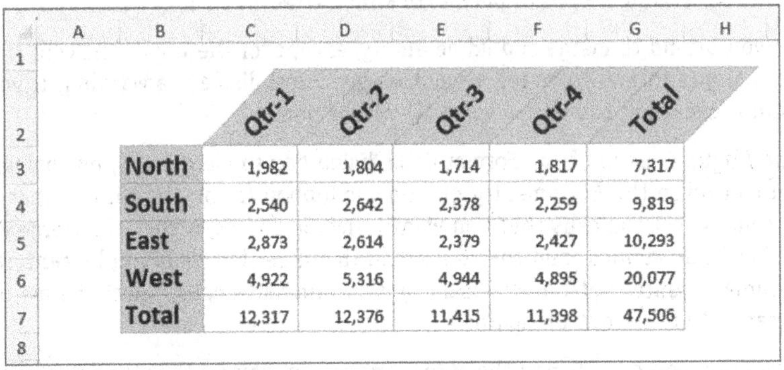

	Qtr-1	Qtr-2	Qtr-3	Qtr-4	Total
North	1,982	1,804	1,714	1,817	7,317
South	2,540	2,642	2,378	2,259	9,819
East	2,873	2,614	2,379	2,427	10,293
West	4,922	5,316	4,944	4,895	20,077
Total	12,317	12,376	11,415	11,398	47,506

You control the color of the cell's text by choosing Home ⇨ Font ⇨ Font Color. Control the cell's background color by choosing Home ⇨ Font ⇨ Fill Color. Both of these color controls are also available on the Mini toolbar, which appears when you right-click a cell or range.

> **TIP**
>
> To hide the contents of a cell, make the background color the same as the font text color. The cell contents are still visible in the Formula bar when you select the cell. Keep in mind, however, that some printers may override this setting, and the text may be visible when printed.

Even though you have access to a lot of colors, you might want to stick with the 10 theme colors (and their light/dark variations) displayed in the various color selection controls. In other words, avoid using the More Colors option, which lets you select a color. Why? First, those 10 colors were chosen because they "go together." (Well, at least somebody thought they did.) Another reason involves document themes. If you switch to a different document theme for your workbook, non-theme colors aren't changed. In some cases, the result may be less than pleasing aesthetically. (See "Understanding Document Themes," later in this chapter, for more information about themes.)

Adding Borders and Lines

Borders (and lines within the borders) are another visual enhancement that you can add around groups of cells. Borders are often used to group a range of similar cells or to delineate rows or columns. Excel offers 13 preset styles of borders, as you can see in the Home ⇨ Font ⇨ Borders drop-down list shown in Figure 9.9. This control works with the selected cell or range and enables you to specify which, if any, border style to use for each border of the selection.

You may prefer to draw borders rather than select a preset border style. To do so, use the Draw Border or Draw Border Grid command from the Home ⇨ Font ⇨ Borders drop-down list. Selecting either command lets you create borders by dragging your mouse. Use the Line Color or Line Style command to change the color or style. When you're finished drawing borders, press Esc to cancel the border-drawing mode.

FIGURE 9.9

Use the Borders drop-down list to add lines around worksheet cells.

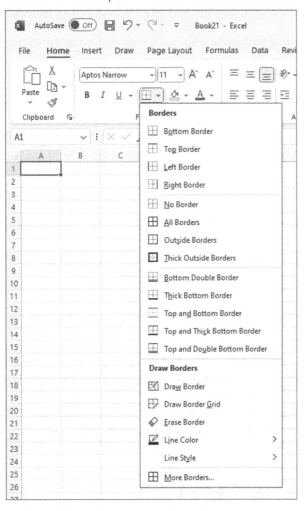

Another way to apply borders is to use the Border tab of the Format Cells dialog box, which is shown in Figure 9.10. One way to display this dialog box is to select More Borders from the Borders drop-down list.

Before you display the Format Cells dialog box, select the cell or range to which you want to add borders. Then, in the Format Cells dialog box, choose a line style and color and then choose the border position for the line style by clicking one or more of the Border icons. (These icons are toggles.)

FIGURE 9.10

Use the Border tab of the Format Cells dialog box for more control over cell borders.

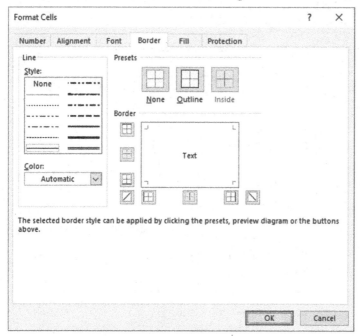

Notice that the Border tab has three preset icons, which can save you some clicking. If you want to remove all borders from the selection, click None. To put an outline around the selection, click Outline. To put borders inside the selection, click Inside.

Excel displays the selected border style in the dialog box; there is no live preview in the worksheet. You can choose different styles for different border positions; you can also choose a color for the border. Using this dialog box may require some experimentation, but you'll get the hang of it.

When you apply two diagonal lines, the cells look like they've been crossed out.

TIP

If you use border formatting in your worksheet, you may want to turn off the grid display to make the borders more pronounced. Choose View ⟳ Show ⟳ Gridlines to toggle the gridline display.

Copying Formats by Painting

Perhaps the quickest way to copy the formats from one cell to another cell or range is to use the Format Painter button (the button with the paintbrush image) of the Home ⇨ Clipboard group.

1. **Select the cell or range that has the formatting attributes that you want to copy.**

2. **Click the Format Painter button.** The mouse pointer changes to include a paintbrush.

3. **Select the cells to which you want to apply the formats.**

4. **Release the mouse button, and Excel applies the same set of formatting options that were in the original range.**

If you double-click the Format Painter button, you can paint multiple areas of the worksheet with the same formats. Excel applies the formats that you copy to each cell or range that you select. To get out of Paint mode, click the Format Painter button again (or press Esc).

Using Named Styles for Easier Formatting

One of the most underutilized features in Excel is named styles. *Named styles* make it easy to apply a set of predefined formatting options to a cell or range. In addition to saving time, using named styles helps to ensure a consistent look.

A style can consist of settings for up to six attributes:

- Number format
- Alignment (vertical and horizontal)
- Font (type, size, and color)
- Borders
- Fill
- Cell protection (locked and hidden)

The real power of styles is apparent when you change a component of a style. All cells that use that named style automatically incorporate the change. Suppose that you apply a particular style to a dozen cells scattered throughout your worksheet. Later, you realize that these cells should have a font size of 14 pt rather than 12 pt. Rather than change each cell, simply edit the style. All cells with that particular style change automatically.

Applying Styles

Excel includes a good selection of predefined named styles that work in conjunction with document themes. Figure 9.11 shows the effect of choosing Home ⇨ Styles ⇨ Cell Styles. Note that this display is a live preview—as you move your mouse over the style choices, the selected cell or range temporarily displays the style. When you see a style you like, click it to apply the style to the selection.

9

FIGURE 9.11

Excel displays samples of predefined cell styles.

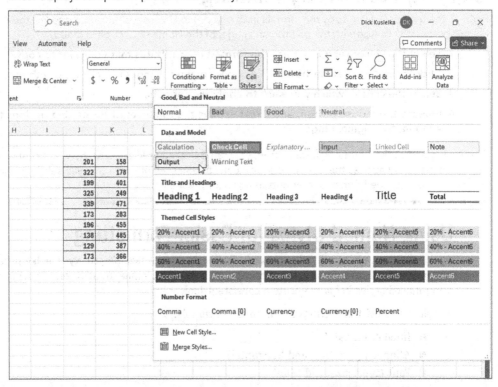

After you apply a style to a cell, you can apply additional formatting to it by using any formatting method discussed in this chapter. Formatting modifications that you make to the cell don't affect other cells that use the same style.

You have quite a bit of control over styles. In fact, you can do any of the following:

- Modify an existing style.
- Create a new style.
- Merge styles from another workbook into the active workbook.

The following sections describe these procedures.

Modifying an Existing Style

To change an existing style, choose Home ⇨ Styles ⇨ Cell Styles. Right-click the style that you want to modify and choose Modify from the context menu. Excel displays the Style dialog box, as shown in Figure 9.12. In this example, the Style dialog box shows the settings for the Office theme Output style. The style definitions vary, depending on which document theme is active.

FIGURE 9.12

Use the Style dialog box to modify named styles.

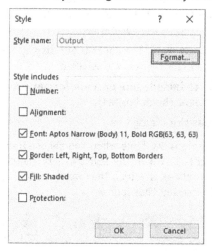

Here's a quick example of how you can use styles to change the default font used throughout your workbook:

1. **Choose Home ⇨ Styles ⇨ Cell Styles.** Excel displays the list of styles for the active workbook.

2. **Right-click Normal and choose Modify.** Excel displays the Style dialog box (refer to Figure 9.12), with the current settings for the Normal style.

3. **Click the Format button.** Excel displays the Format Cells dialog box.

4. **Select the Font tab and choose the font and size that you want as the default.**

5. **Click OK to return to the Style dialog box.** Notice that the Font item displays the font choice you made.

6. **Click OK again to close the Style dialog box.**

The font for all cells that use the Normal style changes to the font that you specified. You can change any formatting attributes for any style.

Creating New Styles

In addition to using Excel's built-in styles, you can create your own styles. This feature enables you to apply your favorite formatting options quickly and consistently.

To create a new style, follow these steps:

1. **Select a cell and apply all the formatting that you want to include in the new style.** You can use any of the formatting that is available in the Format Cells dialog box.

2. **After you format the cell to your liking, choose Home ⇨ Styles ⇨ Cell Styles, and choose New Cell Style.** Excel displays its Style dialog box (refer to Figure 9.12), along with a proposed generic name for the style. Note that Excel displays the words By Example to indicate that it's basing the style on the current cell.

3. **Enter a new style name in the Style Name field.** The check boxes display the current formats for the cell. By default, all check boxes are selected.

4. **(Optional) If you don't want the style to include one or more format categories, remove the check(s) from the appropriate check box(es).**

5. **Click OK to create the style and to close the dialog box.**

After you perform these steps, the new custom style is available when you choose Home ⇨ Styles ⇨ Cell Styles. To delete a custom style, right-click it in the Styles gallery and choose Delete. Custom styles are available only in the workbook in which they were created. To copy your custom styles to another workbook, see the section that follows.

> **NOTE**
> The Protection option in the Style dialog box controls whether users will be able to modify cells for the selected style. This option is effective only if you've also turned on worksheet protection by choosing Review ⇨ Protect ⇨ Protect Sheet.

Merging Styles from Other Workbooks

Custom styles are stored with the workbook in which they were created. If you've created some custom styles, you probably don't want to go through all of the work required to create copies of those styles in each new Excel workbook. A better approach is to merge the styles from a workbook in which you previously created them.

To merge styles from another workbook, open both the workbook that contains the styles that you want to merge and the workbook that will contain the merged styles. Activate the second workbook, choose Home ⇨ Styles ⇨ Cell Styles, and then choose Merge Styles. Excel displays the Merge Styles dialog box that shows a list of all open workbooks. Select the workbook that contains the styles you want to merge and click OK. Excel copies custom styles from the workbook that you selected into the active workbook.

Controlling Styles with Templates

When you start Excel, it loads with several default settings, including the settings for stylistic formatting. If you spend a lot of time changing the default elements for every new workbook, you should know about templates.

Here's an example. You may prefer that gridlines aren't displayed in worksheets. And maybe you prefer Wrap Text to be the default setting for alignment. Templates provide an easy way to change defaults.

The trick is to create a workbook with the Normal style modified in the way you want it. Then save the workbook as a template (with an `.xltx` extension). After doing so, you can choose this template as the basis for a new workbook.

Understanding Document Themes

In an attempt to help users create more professional-looking documents, the Office designers incorporated a feature known as *document themes*. Using themes is an easy (and almost foolproof) way to specify colors, fonts, and a variety of graphic effects in a document. Best of all, changing the entire look of your document is a breeze. A few mouse clicks is all that it takes to apply a different theme and change the look of your workbook.

Importantly, the concept of themes is incorporated into other Office applications. Therefore, a company can easily create a standard and consistent look for all of its documents.

> **NOTE**
>
> Themes don't override specific formatting that you apply. For example, assume that you apply the Accent1 named style to a range. Then you change the font color for a few cells in that range. If you change to a different theme, the manually applied font colors won't be modified to use the new theme font colors. Bottom line: If you plan to take advantage of themes, stick with the default formatting choices.

9

Figure 9.13 shows a worksheet that contains a SmartArt diagram, a table, a chart, and a range formatted with the Title named style, and a range formatted with the Explanatory Text named style. These items all use the default theme, which is the Office theme.

Figure 9.14 shows the same worksheet after applying a different document theme. The different theme changed the fonts, the colors (which may not be apparent in the figure), and the graphics effects for the SmartArt diagram.

FIGURE 9.13

The elements in this worksheet use the default theme.

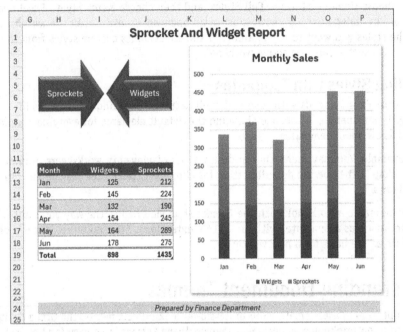

FIGURE 9.14

The worksheet after applying a different theme

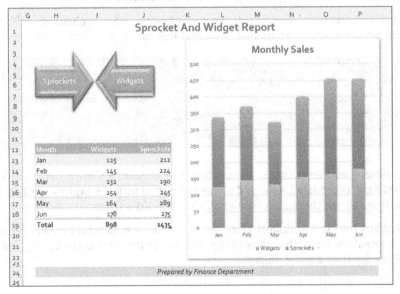

If you'd like to experiment with using various themes, the workbook shown in Figure 9.13 and Figure 9.14 is available on this book's website at www.wiley.com/go/excelquickandeasy. The file is named `theme examples.xlsx`.

Applying a Theme

Figure 9.15 shows the theme choices that appear when you choose Page Layout ⇨ Themes ⇨ Themes. This display is a live preview. As you move your mouse over the theme choices, the active worksheet displays the theme. When you see a theme you like, click it to apply the theme to all worksheets in the workbook.

FIGURE 9.15

Built-in Excel theme choices

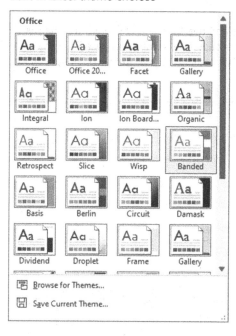

When you specify a particular theme, the gallery choices for various elements reflect the new theme. For example, the chart styles that you can choose from vary, depending on which theme is active.

NOTE

Because themes use different fonts (which can vary in size), changing to a different theme may affect the layout of your worksheet. For example, after you apply a new theme, a worksheet that printed on a single page may spill over to a second page. Therefore, you may need to make some adjustments after you apply a new theme.

Customizing a Theme

Notice that the Themes group on the Page Layout tab contains three other controls: Colors, Fonts, and Effects. You can use these controls to change just one of the three components of a theme. For example, you might like the colors and effects in the Office theme but would prefer different fonts. To change the font set, apply the Office theme and then specify your preferred font set by choosing Page Layout ⇨ Themes ⇨ Fonts.

Each theme uses two fonts (one for headers and one for the body), and in some cases these two fonts are the same. If none of the theme choices is suitable, choose Page Layout ⇨ Themes ⇨ Fonts ⇨ Customize Fonts to specify the two fonts that you prefer (see Figure 9.16).

FIGURE 9.16

Use this dialog box to specify two fonts for a theme.

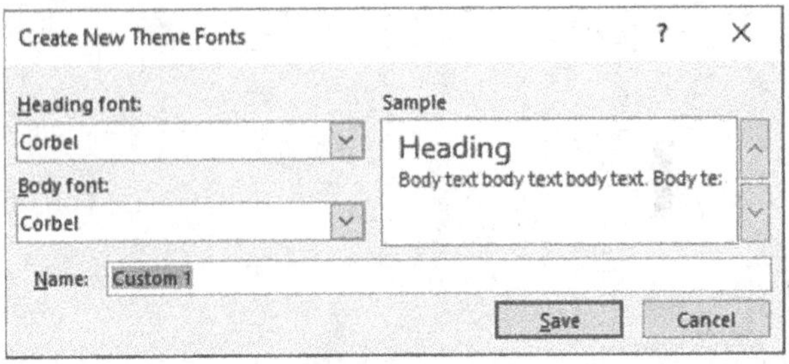

TIP

When you choose Home ⇨ Font ⇨ Font, the two fonts for the current theme are listed first in the drop-down list.

Choose Page Layout ⇨ Themes ⇨ Colors to select a different set of colors. And, if you're so inclined, you can even create a custom set of colors by choosing Page Layout ⇨ Themes ⇨ Colors ⇨ Customize Colors. This command displays the Create New Theme Colors dialog box, as shown in Figure 9.17. Note that each theme consists of 12 colors. Four of the colors are for text and backgrounds, six are for accents, and two are for hyperlinks. As you specify different colors, the preview panel in the dialog box updates.

FIGURE 9.17

If you're feeling creative, you can specify a set of custom colors for a theme.

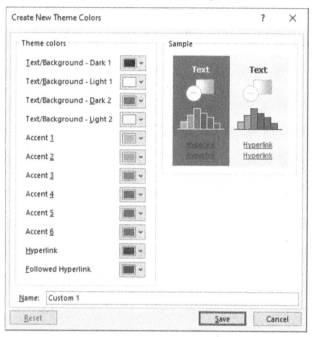

If you've customized a theme using different fonts or colors, you can save the new theme by choosing Page Layout ➪ Themes ➪ Save Current Theme. Your customized themes appear in the Themes list in the Custom category. Other Office applications, such as Word and Power-Point, can use these theme files. If you need to delete your custom theme, right-click it in the Themes gallery and choose Delete.

9

Using Conditional Formatting

You can apply *conditional formatting* to a cell so that the cell looks different depending on its contents. Conditional formatting is a useful tool for visualizing numeric data. In some cases, conditional formatting may be a viable alternative to creating a chart. This chapter covers how to specify conditional formatting, including formatting using graphics, and creating rules for conditional formatting. The chapter also shows conditional formatting examples and steps for performing other formatting tasks.

Specifying Conditional Formatting

Conditional formatting lets you apply cell formatting selectively and automatically, based on the contents of the cells. For example, you can apply conditional formatting in such a way that all negative values in a range have a light-yellow background color. When you enter or change a value in the range, Excel applies the conditional formatting rules for the cell. If the value is negative, the background is shaded; otherwise, no formatting is applied.

To apply a conditional formatting rule to a cell or range, select the cells and then use one of the commands from the Home ⇨ Styles ⇨ Conditional Formatting drop-down list to specify a rule. The choices are as follows:

- **Highlight Cells Rules:** Examples include highlighting cells that are greater than a particular value, are between two values, contain a specific text string, contain a date, or are duplicated.
- **Top/Bottom Rules:** Examples include highlighting the top 10 items, the items in the bottom 20%, and the items that are above average.
- **Data Bars:** Applies graphic bars directly in the cells, proportional to the cell's value.
- **Color Scales:** Applies background color, proportional to the cell's value.

- **Icon Sets:** Displays icons directly in the cells. The icons depend on the cell's value.
- **New Rule:** Enables you to specify other conditional formatting rules, including rules based on a logical formula.
- **Clear Rules:** Deletes all the conditional formatting rules from the selected cells.
- **Manage Rules:** Displays the Conditional Formatting Rules Manager dialog box in which you create new conditional formatting rules, edit rules, or delete rules.

Using Graphical Conditional Formats

The following sections describe the three conditional formatting options that display graphics: data bars, color scales, and icon sets. These types of conditional formatting can be useful for visualizing the values in a range.

Using Data Bars

The data bars conditional format displays horizontal bars directly in the cell. The length of the bar is based on the value of the cell relative to the other values in the range.

Figure 10.1 shows an example of data bars. It's a list of tracks on a number of Bob Dylan albums, with the length of each track in column D. With data bar conditional formatting applied to column D, you can tell at a glance which tracks are longer.

FIGURE 10.1

The length of the data bars is proportional to the track length in the cell in column D.

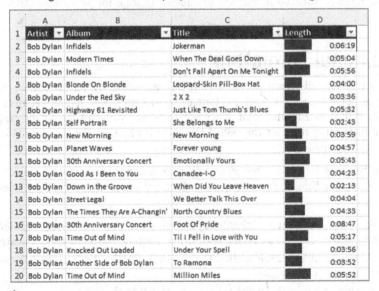

	A	B	C	D
1	Artist	Album	Title	Length
2	Bob Dylan	Infidels	Jokerman	0:06:19
3	Bob Dylan	Modern Times	When The Deal Goes Down	0:05:04
4	Bob Dylan	Infidels	Don't Fall Apart On Me Tonight	0:05:56
5	Bob Dylan	Blonde On Blonde	Leopard-Skin Pill-Box Hat	0:04:00
6	Bob Dylan	Under the Red Sky	2 X 2	0:03:36
7	Bob Dylan	Highway 61 Revisited	Just Like Tom Thumb's Blues	0:05:32
8	Bob Dylan	Self Portrait	She Belongs to Me	0:02:43
9	Bob Dylan	New Morning	New Morning	0:03:59
10	Bob Dylan	Planet Waves	Forever young	0:04:57
11	Bob Dylan	30th Anniversary Concert	Emotionally Yours	0:05:43
12	Bob Dylan	Good As I Been to You	Canadee-I-O	0:04:23
13	Bob Dylan	Down in the Groove	When Did You Leave Heaven	0:02:13
14	Bob Dylan	Street Legal	We Better Talk This Over	0:04:04
15	Bob Dylan	The Times They Are A-Changin'	North Country Blues	0:04:33
16	Bob Dylan	30th Anniversary Concert	Foot Of Pride	0:08:47
17	Bob Dylan	Time Out of Mind	Til I Fell in Love with You	0:05:17
18	Bob Dylan	Knocked Out Loaded	Under Your Spell	0:03:56
19	Bob Dylan	Another Side of Bob Dylan	To Ramona	0:03:52
20	Bob Dylan	Time Out of Mind	Million Miles	0:05:52

 The examples in this section are available on this book's website at www.wiley.com/go/ excelquickandeasy. The workbook is named data bars examples.xlsx.

TIP

When you adjust the column width, the bar lengths adjust accordingly. The differences among the bar lengths are more prominent when the column is wider.

Excel provides quick access to 12 data bar styles via Home ➪ Styles ➪ Conditional Formatting ➪ Data Bars. For additional choices, click the More Rules option, which displays the New Formatting Rule dialog box. Use this dialog box to do the following:

- Show the bar only. (Hide the numbers.)
- Specify Minimum and Maximum values for the scaling.
- Change the appearance of the bars.
- Specify how negative values and the axis are handled.
- Specify the direction of the bars.

Using Color Scales

The color scale conditional formatting option varies the background color of a cell based on the cell's value relative to other cells in the range.

Figure 10.2 shows examples of color scale conditional formatting. The example on the left depicts monthly sales for three regions. Conditional formatting was applied to the range B4:D15. The conditional formatting uses a three-color scale, with red for the lowest value, yellow for the midpoint, and green for the highest value (in Figure 10.2, the red that appears in Excel is the darkest, yellow is the lightest, and green is between those two). Values in between are displayed using a color within the gradient. It's clear that the Central region consistently has lower sales volumes, but the conditional formatting doesn't help identify monthly differences for a particular region.

FIGURE 10.2

Two examples of color scale conditional formatting

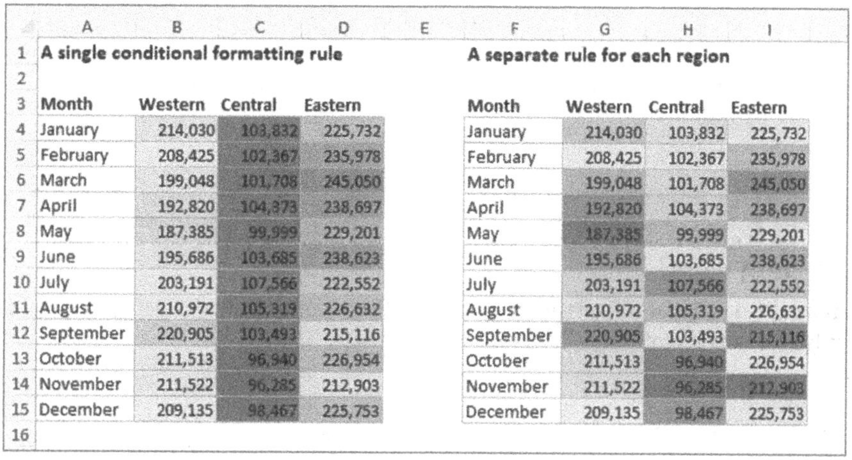

	A	B	C	D	E	F	G	H	I
1	**A single conditional formatting rule**					**A separate rule for each region**			
2									
3	Month	Western	Central	Eastern		Month	Western	Central	Eastern
4	January	214,030	103,832	225,732		January	214,030	103,832	225,732
5	February	208,425	102,367	235,978		February	208,425	102,367	235,978
6	March	199,048	101,708	245,050		March	199,048	101,708	245,050
7	April	192,820	104,373	238,697		April	192,820	104,373	238,697
8	May	187,385	99,999	229,201		May	187,385	99,999	229,201
9	June	195,686	103,685	238,623		June	195,686	103,685	238,623
10	July	203,191	107,566	222,552		July	203,191	107,566	222,552
11	August	210,972	105,319	226,632		August	210,972	105,319	226,632
12	September	220,905	103,493	215,116		September	220,905	103,493	215,116
13	October	211,513	96,940	226,954		October	211,513	96,940	226,954
14	November	211,522	96,285	212,903		November	211,522	96,285	212,903
15	December	209,135	98,467	225,753		December	209,135	98,467	225,753
16									

The example on the right shows the same data, but conditional formatting was applied to each region separately. This approach facilitates comparisons within a region and can identify high or low sales months.

Neither one of these approaches is necessarily better. The way you set up conditional formatting depends entirely on what you're trying to visualize.

This workbook, named color scale example.xlsx, is available on this book's website at www.wiley.com/go/excelquickandeasy.

Excel provides six two-color scale presets and six three-color scale presets, which you can apply to the selected range by choosing Home ⇨ Styles ⇨ Conditional Formatting ⇨ Color Scales.

To customize the colors and other options, choose Home ⇨ Styles ⇨ Conditional Formatting ⇨ Color Scales ⇨ More Rules, and the New Formatting Rule dialog box, shown in Figure 10.3, appears. Adjust the settings and watch the Preview box to see the effects of your changes.

FIGURE 10.3

Use the New Formatting Rule dialog box to customize a color scale.

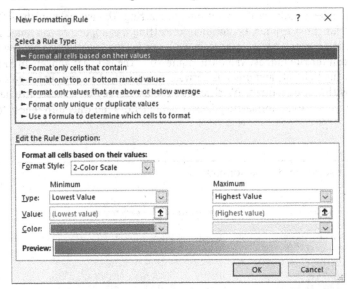

Using Icon Sets

Yet another conditional formatting option is to display an icon in the cell. The icon displayed depends on the value of the cell.

To assign an icon set to a range, select the cells and choose Home ⇨ Styles ⇨ Conditional Formatting ⇨ Icon Sets. Excel provides 20 icon sets from which you may choose. The number of icons in the sets ranges from three to five. You can't create a custom icon set.

Figure 10.4 shows an example that uses an icon set. The symbols graphically depict the status of each project, based on the value in column C.

FIGURE 10.4

Using an icon set to indicate the status of projects

	A	B	C	D
1		Project Status Report		
2				
3		Project	Pct Completed	
4		Project 1	95%	
5		Project 2	100%	
6		Project 3	50%	
7		Project 4	0%	
8		Project 5	20%	
9		Project 6	80%	
10		Project 7	100%	
11		Project 8	0%	
12		Project 9	0%	
13		Project 10	50%	
14				

 The icon set example in this section is available on this book's website at www.wiley.com/go/excelquickandeasy. The workbook is named icon set examples.xlsx.

By default, the symbols are assigned using percentiles. The data is split into the same number of groups as there are icons in the icon set applied: three, four, or five.

If you would like more control over how the icons are assigned, choose Home ⇨ Styles ⇨ Conditional Formatting ⇨ Icon Sets ⇨ More Rules to display the New Formatting Rule dialog box. To modify an existing rule, choose Home ⇨ Styles ⇨ Conditional Formatting ⇨ Manage Rules. Then select the rule to modify and click the Edit Rule button.

Figure 10.5 shows how to modify the icon set rules such that only projects that are 100% complete get the check mark icons. Projects that are 0% complete get the X icon. All other projects get no icon.

Figure 10.6 shows the project status list after making this change.

10

FIGURE 10.5

Changing the icon assignment rule

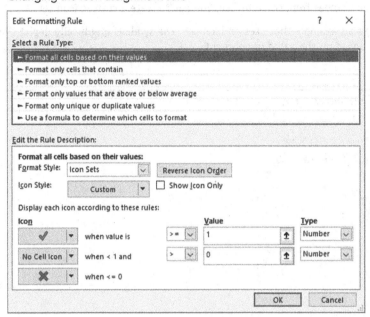

FIGURE 10.6

Using a modified rule and eliminating an icon makes the table more readable.

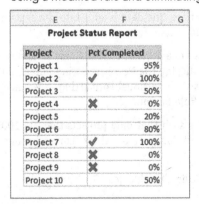

Creating Formula-Based Rules

The graphical conditional formats are generally used to show a cell in relation to other, nearby cells. Formula-based rules generally apply to one cell independently. The same rule may apply to many cells, but each cell is considered on its own.

The Highlight Cells Rules and Top/Bottom Rules options under the Conditional Formatting Ribbon control are commonly used shortcuts for formula-based rules. If you choose Home ⇨ Styles ⇨ Conditional Formatting ⇨ New Rule, Excel displays the New Formatting Rule dialog box. You saw this dialog box in the previous section when the built-in graphical conditional formats needed tweaking. The entry Format Only Cells That Contain is another shortcut for a formula-based rule.

The last entry in the New Formatting Rule dialog box is Use A Formula To Determine Which Cells To Format. This is the entry you choose if none of the other shortcuts do what you want. It provides maximum flexibility for creating a rule.

NOTE

The formula must return either TRUE or FALSE. If the formula evaluates to TRUE, the condition is satisfied and the conditional formatting is applied. If the formula evaluates to FALSE, the conditional formatting is not applied.

 A workbook with examples from this section is available on this book's website at www.wiley.com/go/ excelquickandeasy. The file is named conditional formatting formulas.xlsx.

Understanding Relative and Absolute References

If the formula that you enter into the New Formatting Rule or Edit Formatting Rule dialog box contains a cell reference, that reference is considered a relative reference based on the upper-left cell in the selected range.

For example, suppose that you want to set up a conditional formatting condition that applies shading to cells in range A1:B10 only if the cell contains text. None of Excel's conditional formatting options can do this task, so you need to create a formula that will return TRUE if the cell contains text and FALSE otherwise. Follow these steps (see Figure 10.7):

1. **Select the range A1:B10, and make sure that cell A1 is the active cell.**
2. **Choose Home ⇨ Styles ⇨ Conditional Formatting ⇨ New Rule.** The New Formatting Rule dialog box appears.
3. **Click the Use a Formula to Determine Which Cells To Format rule type.**
4. **Enter the following formula into the Formula box:**

   =ISTEXT(A1)

5. **Click the Format button.** The Format Cells dialog box appears.
6. **From the Fill tab, specify the cell shading that will be applied if the formula returns** TRUE.
7. **Click OK to return to the New Formatting Rule dialog box** (see Figure 10.7).
8. **Click OK to close the New Formatting Rule dialog box.**

10

FIGURE 10.7

Creating a conditional formatting rule based on a formula

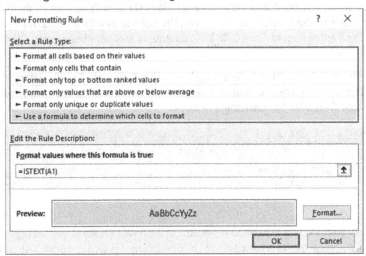

Notice that the formula entered in step 4 contains a relative reference to the upper-left cell in the selected range.

Generally, when entering a conditional formatting formula for a range of cells, you'll use a reference to the active cell, which is typically the upper-left cell in the selected range. One exception is when you need to refer to a specific cell. For example, suppose that you select range A1:B10 and you want to apply formatting to all cells in the range that exceed the value in cell C1. Enter this conditional formatting formula:

```
=A1>$C$1
```

In this case, the reference to cell C1 is an absolute reference; it will not be adjusted for the cells in the selected range. In other words, the conditional formatting formula for cell A2 looks like this:

```
=A2>$C$1
```

The relative cell reference is adjusted, but the absolute cell reference is not.

Conditional Formatting Formula Examples

Each of these examples uses a formula entered directly into the New Formatting Rule dialog box after the Use A Formula To Determine Which Cells To Format rule type is selected. You decide the type of formatting that you apply conditionally.

Identifying Weekend Days

Excel provides a number of conditional formatting rules that deal with dates, but it doesn't let you identify dates that fall on a weekend. Use this formula to identify weekend dates:

```
=OR(WEEKDAY(A1)=7,WEEKDAY(A1)=1)
```

This formula assumes that a range is selected and that cell A1 is the active cell.

Highlighting a Row Based on a Value

Figure 10.8 shows part of a worksheet that contains a conditional formula in the range A3:G28. If a name entered in cell B1 is found in the first column, the entire row for that name is highlighted.

FIGURE 10.8

Highlighting a row, based on a matching name

	A	B	C	D	E	F	G	H
1	Name:	Noel						
2								
3	Alice	7	118	61	55	85	26	
4	Bob	198	134	180	3	132	63	
5	Carl	2	46	59	63	59	26	
6	Denise	190	121	12	26	68	97	
7	Elvin	174	42	176	68	124	14	
8	Francis	129	114	83	103	129	129	
9	George	9	128	24	44	139	108	
10	Harald	168	183	200	167	134	83	
11	Ivan	165	141	95	91	100	144	
12	June	116	171	109	84	148	15	
13	Kathy	131	43	197	82	103	163	
14	Larry	139	30	171	122	34	196	
15	Mary	31	171	185	162	171	17	
16	Noel	78	126	190	78	123	2	
17	Oliver	157	98	100	75	137	10	
18	Patrick	120	144	106	39	39	119	
19	Quincey	156	200	58	74	37	76	
20	Raul	58	147	160	182	11	79	

The conditional formatting formula is as follows:

```
=$A3=$B$1
```

Notice that a mixed reference is used for cell A3. Because the column part of the reference is absolute, the comparison is always done using the contents of column A.

Displaying Alternate-Row Shading

The conditional formatting formula that follows was applied to the range A1:D18, as shown in Figure 10.9, to apply shading to alternate rows:

```
=MOD(ROW(),2)=0
```

FIGURE 10.9

Using conditional formatting to apply formatting to alternate rows

	A	B	C	D	E
1	812	546	866	866	
2	546	232	946	946	
3	102	489	187	712	
4	63	423	497	615	
5	624	370	456	201	
6	850	910	575	960	
7	996	35	375	412	
8	993	24	727	263	
9	985	198	558	305	
10	709	549	150	343	
11	354	125	439	568	
12	900	474	717	177	
13	913	614	638	56	
14	950	904	948	15	
15	92	7	779	876	
16	841	496	278	911	
17	10	59	986	836	
18	608	817	238	594	
19					

Alternate row shading can make your spreadsheets easier to read. If you add or delete rows within the conditional formatting area, the shading is updated automatically.

This formula uses the ROW function (which returns the row number) and the MOD function (which returns the remainder of its first argument divided by its second argument). For cells in even-numbered rows, the MOD function returns 0, and cells in that row are formatted.

For alternate shading of columns, use the COLUMN function instead of the ROW function.

Creating Checkerboard Shading

The following formula is a variation on the example in the preceding section. It applies formatting to alternate rows and columns, creating a checkerboard effect:

```
=MOD(ROW(),2)=MOD(COLUMN(),2)
```

Shading Groups of Rows

Here's another row-shading variation. The following formula shades alternate groups of rows. It produces four shaded rows, followed by four unshaded rows, followed by four more shaded rows, and so on.

```
=MOD(INT((ROW()-1)/4)+1,2)=1
```

Figure 10.10 shows an example.

FIGURE 10.10

Conditional formatting produces these groups of alternating shaded rows.

	A	B	C	D	E
1	494	460	493	143	
2	450	154	149	375	
3	168	358	128	259	
4	75	163	339	18	
5	64	365	466	383	
6	457	40	86	393	
7	481	41	177	280	
8	273	402	367	82	
9	66	91	500	398	
10	3	187	403	15	
11	244	210	458	186	
12	197	96	379	320	
13	477	314	332	29	
14	243	465	249	350	
15	54	324	228	360	
16	119	124	248	198	
17	162	114	207	312	
18	23	195	267	475	
19	71	244	285	75	
20	238	1	323	92	
21	496	338	232	372	
22	65	195	102	317	
23					

For different-sized groups, change the 4 to some other value. For example, use this formula to shade alternate groups of two rows:

```
=MOD(INT((ROW()-1)/2)+1,2)=1
```

Working with Conditional Formats

The following sections describe some additional information about conditional formatting that you may find useful.

Managing Rules

The Conditional Formatting Rules Manager dialog box is useful for checking, editing, deleting, and adding conditional formats. First, select any cell in the range that contains conditional formatting. Then choose Home ⇨ Styles ⇨ Conditional Formatting ⇨ Manage Rules.

You can specify as many rules as you like by clicking the New Rule button. Cells can even use data bars, color scales, and icon sets at the same time.

10

Copying Cells That Contain Conditional Formatting

Conditional formatting information is stored with a cell much like standard formatting information is stored with a cell. As a result, when you copy a cell that contains conditional formatting, you also copy the conditional formatting.

> **TIP**
>
> To copy only the formatting (including conditional formatting), copy the cells and then use the Paste Special dialog box and select the Formats option, or choose Home ➪ Clipboard ➪ Paste ➪ Formatting (R).

If you insert rows or columns within a range that contains conditional formatting, the new cells have the same conditional formatting.

Deleting Conditional Formatting

When you press Delete to delete the contents of a cell, you don't delete the conditional formatting (if any) for the cell. To remove all conditional formats (as well as all other cell formatting), select the cell and then choose Home ➪ Editing ➪ Clear ➪ Clear Formats. Or choose Home ➪ Editing ➪ Clear ➪ Clear All to delete the cell contents and the conditional formatting.

To remove only conditional formatting (and leave the other formatting intact), choose Home ➪ Styles ➪ Conditional Formatting ➪ Clear Rules and choose one of the available options.

Locating Cells That Contain Conditional Formatting

You can't always tell, just by looking at a cell, whether it contains conditional formatting. You can, however, use the Go To Special dialog box to select such cells.

1. **Choose Home ➪ Editing ➪ Find & Select ➪ Go To Special.** The Go To Special dialog box appears.
2. **In the Go To Special dialog box, select the Conditional Formats option.**
3. **To select all cells on the worksheet containing conditional formatting, select the All option.** To select only the cells that contain the same conditional formatting as the active cell, select the Same option.
4. **Click OK. Excel selects the cells for you.**

> **NOTE**
>
> The Excel Find And Replace dialog box includes a feature that allows you to search your worksheet to locate cells that contain specific formatting. This feature does not locate cells that contain formatting resulting from conditional formatting.

Getting Started with Excel Charts

IN THIS CHAPTER

- How Excel handles charts
- The parts of a chart
- The basic steps for creating a chart
- Working with charts

C harts offer a visual representation of numeric values; they are at-a-glance views that allow you to specify relationships between data values, point out differences, and observe business trends. Few mechanisms allow you to absorb data faster than a chart, which can be a key component in your dashboard.

When most people think of a spreadsheet product such as Excel, they think of crunching rows and columns of numbers. But Excel also has a plethora of tools to present data visually in the form of a chart. In this chapter, we present an overview of Excel's charting capabilities and show you how to create and customize your own charts using Excel.

 The sample workbook for this chapter (Intro to Charts.xlsx) can be found at www.wiley .com/go/excelquickandeasy.

What Is a Chart?

A *chart* is a visual representation of numeric values. Charts (also known as *graphs*) have been an integral part of spreadsheets since the early days of Lotus 1-2-3. Charts generated by early spreadsheet products were extremely crude by today's standards. Over the years, however, the quality and flexibility have improved significantly. You'll find that Excel provides you with the tools to create a wide variety of highly customizable charts that can help you effectively communicate your message.

Displaying data in a well-conceived chart can make your numbers more understandable. Because a chart presents a picture, they are particularly useful for summarizing a series of numbers and their interrelationships. Making a chart can often help you spot trends and patterns that might otherwise go unnoticed.

Figure 11.1 shows a worksheet that contains a simple column chart that depicts a company's sales volume by month. Viewing the chart makes it apparent that sales were off in the summer months (June through August), but they increased steadily during the final four months of the year. You could, of course, arrive at this same conclusion simply by studying the numbers. But viewing the chart makes the point much more quickly. A column chart is just one of many different types of charts that you can create with Excel.

FIGURE 11.1

A simple column chart depicts the sales volume for each month.

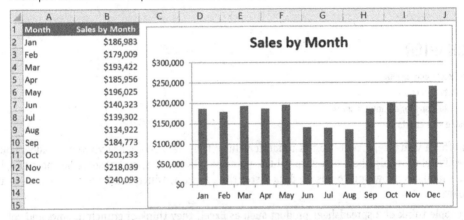

How Excel Handles Charts

Before you can create a chart, you must have some numbers (data). The data, of course, is stored in the cells in a worksheet. Normally, the data that is used by a chart resides in a single worksheet, but that's not a strict requirement. A chart can use data that's stored in any number of worksheets, and the worksheets can even be in different workbooks. The decision to use data from one sheet or multiple sheets really depends on your data model, the nature of your data sources, and the interactivity that you want to give your dashboard.

A chart is essentially an "object" that Excel creates upon request. This object consists of one or more *data series* (or set of data), displayed graphically. The appearance of the data series depends on the selected *chart type*. For example, if you create a line chart that uses two data series, the chart contains two lines, and each line represents one data series. The data for each series is stored in a separate row or column. Each point on the line is determined by the value in a single cell and is represented by a marker. You can distinguish the lines by their thickness, line style, color, or data markers.

Figure 11.2 shows a line chart that plots two data series across a nine-year period. The series are identified by using different data markers (squares versus circles), shown in the *legend* at the bottom of the chart. The lines also use different colors, which is not apparent in the gray-scale figure.

FIGURE 11.2

This line chart displays two data series.

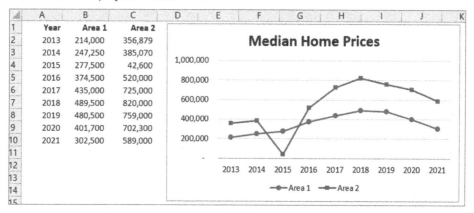

A key point to keep in mind is that charts are dynamic. In other words, a chart series is linked to the data in your worksheet. If the data changes, the chart is updated automatically to reflect those changes so that your dashboard can show the most current information.

After you've created a chart, you can always change its type, change the formatting, add new data series to it, or change an existing data series so that it uses data in a different range.

Embedded Charts

An *embedded chart* basically floats on top of a worksheet, on the worksheet's drawing layer. The charts shown previously in this chapter are both embedded charts.

As with other drawing objects (such as a text box or a shape), you can move an embedded chart, resize it, change its proportions, adjust its borders, and add effects such as a shadow. Using an embedded chart enables you to view the chart next to the data that it uses. Alternatively, you can place several embedded charts together so that they print on a single page.

When you create a chart, it always starts off as an embedded chart. The exception to this rule is when you select a range of data and press F11 to create a default chart. Such a chart is created on a chart sheet.

To make any changes to the actual chart in an embedded chart object, you must click it to *activate* the chart. When a chart is activated, Excel displays the two contextual tabs shown in Figure 11.3: Chart Design and Format.

FIGURE 11.3

Activating a chart displays additional tabs on the Excel Ribbon.

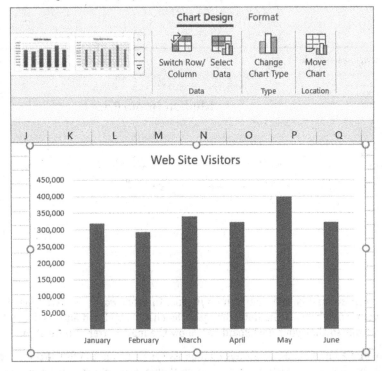

Chart Sheets

You can move an embedded chart to its own chart sheet so that you can view it by clicking a sheet tab. When you move a chart to a chart sheet, the chart occupies the entire sheet. If you plan to print a chart on a page by itself, using a chart sheet is often your better choice. If you have many charts to create, you may want to put each one on a separate chart sheet to avoid cluttering your worksheet. This technique also makes locating a particular chart easier because you can change the name of each chart sheet's tab to an easy-to-find, relevant name. Although chart sheets are not typically used in traditional dashboards, they can come in handy when producing reports that will be viewed in a multi-tab workbook.

Figure 11.4 illustrates a chart sheet. Note the only object on a chart sheet is the chart itself; there is no worksheet area.

FIGURE 11.4

A chart on a chart sheet

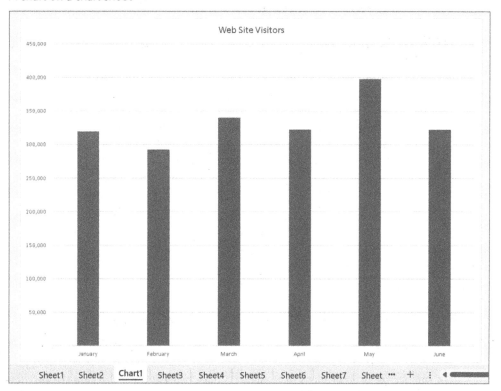

11

Parts of a Chart

A chart is made up of many different elements, and all these elements are optional. Yes, you can create a chart that contains no chart elements—an empty chart. It's not very useful, but Excel allows it.

Refer to the chart in Figure 11.5 as you read the following description of the chart's elements.

This particular chart is a combination chart that displays both columns and a line. The chart has two data series: Income and Profit. Income is plotted as vertical columns, and Profit is plotted as a line. Each bar represents a single *data point* (the value in a cell).

The chart has a horizontal axis, known as the *category axis*. This axis represents the category for each data point (January, February, and so on). This axis doesn't have a label because the category units are obvious.

Notice that this chart has two vertical axes. These are known as *value axes*, and each one has a different scale. The axis on the left is for the column series (Income), and the secondary axis on the right is for the line series (Profit).

Both vertical axes also display scale values. The axis on the left displays scale values from 0 to 200,000, in major unit increments of 20,000. The value axis on the right uses a different scale: 0 percent to 12 percent, in increments of 2 percent.

FIGURE 11.5

Parts of a chart

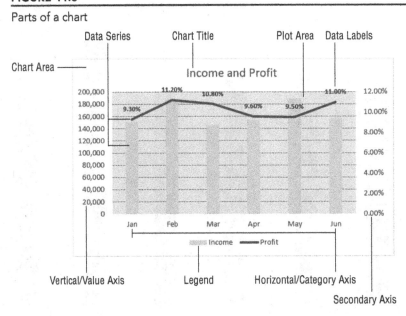

It's appropriate that the chart in Figure 11.5 have two value axes because the two data series vary dramatically in scale. If the Profit Margin data was plotted using the left axis, the line would not even be visible.

If a chart has more than one data series, you'll usually need a way to identify the data series or data points. A legend, for example, is often used to identify the various series in a chart. In this example, the legend appears at the bottom of the chart. Some charts also display data labels to identify specific data points. The example chart displays data labels for the Profit series, but not for the Income series. In addition, most charts (including the example chart) contain a chart title and additional labels to identify the axes or categories.

The example chart also contains horizontal gridlines (which correspond to the values on the left axis). Gridlines are basically extensions of the value axis scale, which makes it easier for the viewer to determine the magnitude of the data points.

In addition, all charts have a *chart area* (the entire background area of the chart) and a *plot area* (the part that shows the actual chart, including the plotted data, the axes, and the axis labels).

Charts can have additional parts or fewer parts, depending on the chart type. For example, a pie chart (see Figure 11.6) has "slices" and no axes. A 3D chart may have *walls* and a *floor* (see Figure 11.7).

Several other types of items can be added to a chart. For example, you can add a *trend line* or display *error bars*.

FIGURE 11.6

A pie chart

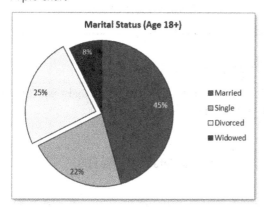

FIGURE 11.7

A 3D column chart

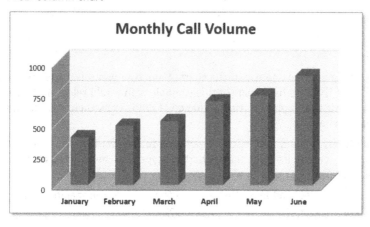

Chart Limitations

As with most features in Excel, charts do have limits on the amount of data that they can handle and present. Table 11.1 lists the limitations of Excel charts.

TABLE 11.1 **Limitations of Excel charts**

Item	Limitation
Charts in a worksheet	Limited by available memory
Worksheets referred to by a chart	255
Data series in a chart	255
Data points in a data series	Limited by available memory
Data points in a data series (3D charts)	Limited by available memory
Total data points in a chart	Limited by available memory

Basic Steps for Creating a Chart

Creating a chart is relatively easy. This section describes how to create and then customize a basic chart to best communicate your business goals.

Creating the Chart

Follow these general steps to create a chart using the data in Figure 11.8:

FIGURE 11.8

This data would make a good chart.

◢	A	B	C
1		Projected	Actual
2	Jan	2,000	1,895
3	Feb	2,500	2,643
4	Mar	3,500	3,648

1. Select the data you want to use in the chart. Make sure you select the column and/or row headers if the data has them (in this example, you would select A1:C4). Another option is to select a single cell within a range of data. Excel then uses the entire data range for the chart.

2. Select the Insert tab and then click a Chart icon in the Charts group. The icon expands into a gallery list that shows chart subtypes for the selected chart type (see Figure 11.9).

3. Click a Chart subtype, and Excel then creates the chart of the specified type. Figure 11.10 shows a column chart created from the data.

Switching the Row and Column Orientation

When Excel creates a chart, it uses an algorithm to determine whether the data appears in columns or in rows. Most of the time Excel guesses correctly, but if it creates the chart using the wrong orientation, you can quickly change it by selecting the chart and choosing Chart Design

⇨ Data ⇨ Switch Row/Column. This command is a toggle, so if changing the data orientation doesn't improve the chart, just choose the command again (or click the Undo button found on the Quick Access Toolbar).

FIGURE 11.9

The icons in the Charts group expand to show a gallery of chart subtypes.

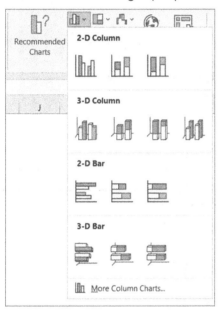

The orientation of the data has a drastic effect on the look (and, perhaps, the understand-ability) of your chart. Figure 11.11 shows the column chart in Figure 11.10 after changing the orientation. Notice that the chart now has three data series, one for each month. If the goal of your dashboard is to compare actual with projected values for each month, this version of the chart is much more difficult to interpret because the relevant columns are not adjacent.

Changing the Chart Type

After you've created a chart, you can easily change the chart type. Although a column chart may work well for a particular dataset, there's no harm in checking out some other chart types. You can choose Chart Design ⇨ Type ⇨ Change Chart Type to display the Change Chart Type dialog box and experiment with other chart types. Figure 11.12 shows the Change Chart Type dialog box.

FIGURE 11.10

A column chart with two data series

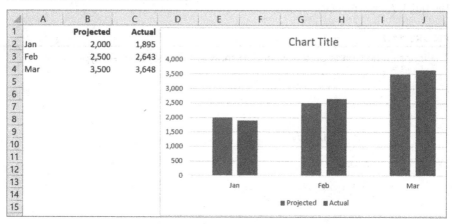

FIGURE 11.11

The column chart, after swapping the row/column orientation

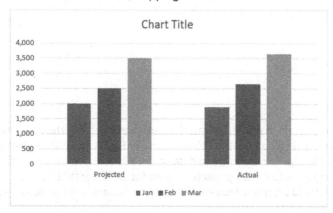

NOTE

If your chart uses more than one data series, make sure that a chart element other than a data series is selected when you choose the Chart Design ⇔ Type ⇔ Change Chart Type command. If you select a series, the command changes the chart type of the selected series only.

In the Change Chart Type dialog box, the main categories are listed on the left, and the sub-types are shown as icons. Select an icon and click OK, and Excel displays the chart using the new chart type. If you don't like the result, click the Undo button.

FIGURE 11.12

The Change Chart Type dialog box

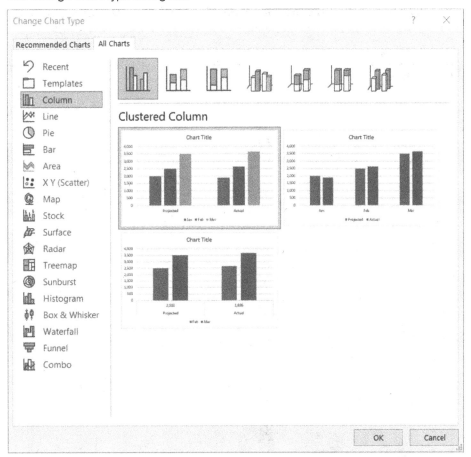

Applying a Chart Layout

Each chart type has a number of prebuilt layouts that you can apply with a single mouse click. A layout contains additional chart elements, such as a title, data labels, axes, and so on. This step is optional, but one of the prebuilt designs might be just what you need.

Even if the layout isn't exactly what you want, it may be close enough that you need to make only a few adjustments.

To apply a layout, select the chart and choose Chart Design ⇨ Chart Layouts ⇨ Quick Layout Gallery. Figure 11.13 shows how a column chart would look using various layouts.

FIGURE 11.13

One-click design variations of a column chart

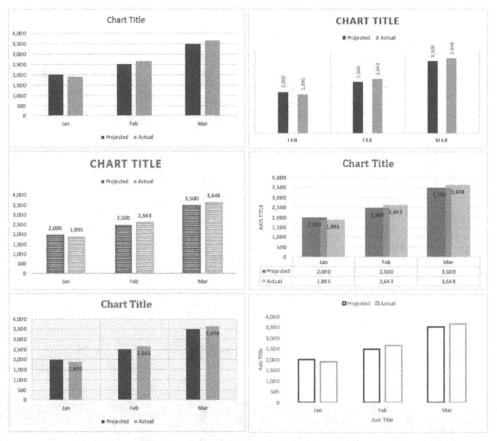

Applying a Chart Style

The Chart Design ⇨ Chart Styles gallery contains quite a few styles that you can apply to your chart. The styles consist of various color choices and some special effects. Again, this step is optional.

> **TIP**
>
> The styles displayed in the gallery depend on the workbook's theme. When you choose Page Layout ⟿ Themes to apply a different theme, you'll see a new selection of chart styles designed for the selected theme.

Adding and Deleting Chart Elements

In some cases, applying a chart layout or chart style (as described previously) gives you a chart with all of the elements that you need. Most of the time, however, you'll need to add or remove some chart elements and fine-tune the layout. You do this using the controls on the Chart Design and Format tabs.

For example, to give a chart a title, click the chart, then choose Chart Design ⟿ Chart Layouts ⟿ Add Chart Element ⟿ Chart Title. The control displays some options that determine where the title is placed. Excel inserts a title with the text "Chart Title." Double-click the text and replace it with your actual chart title.

Formatting Chart Elements

Every element in a chart can be formatted and customized in many ways. Many users are content with charts that are created using the steps described earlier in this chapter. Because you're reading this book, however, you probably want to find out how to customize charts for maximum impact.

Excel provides two ways to format and customize individual chart elements. Each of the following methods requires that you select the chart element first:

- Click the target chart element and then use the Ribbon controls on the Format tab.
- Click the chart element and then press Ctrl+1 to display the Format task pane that's specific to the selected chart element.

You can also double-click a chart element to display the Format task pane for the element.

Assume that you'd like to change the color of the columns for one of the series in the chart. Click any column in the series (which selects the entire series). Then choose Format ⟿ Shape Styles ⟿ Shape Fill and choose a color from the displayed list.

To change the properties of the outline around the columns, choose Format ⟿ Shape Styles ⟿ Shape Outline.

To change the effects used in the columns (e.g., to add a shadow), choose Format ⟿ Shape Styles ⟿ Shape Effects.

Alternatively, you can select a series in the chart, press Ctrl+1, and use the Format Data Series task pane, as shown in Figure 11.14.

FIGURE 11.14

Using the Format Data Series task pane

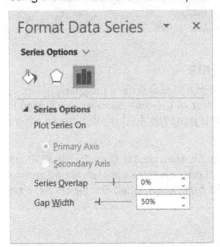

Notice the icons in Figure 11.14. These icons are essentially tabs that expose various formatting options. Click an icon along the top and then expand any of the given sections to view additional controls. It's also a docked pane, so you can adjust multiple elements in the chart and see the changes you specify in real time.

Modifying and Customizing Charts

This section covers common chart modifications.

> **NOTE**
>
> Before you can modify a chart, you must activate it. To activate an embedded chart, click it, which also selects the element that you click. To activate a chart on a chart sheet, just click its sheet tab.

Moving and Resizing a Chart

If your chart is an embedded chart, you can freely move and resize it with your mouse. Click the chart's border and then drag the border to move the chart. Drag any of the eight "handles" to resize the chart. The handles consist of white circles that appear on the chart's corners and edges when you click the chart's border. When the mouse pointer turns into a double arrow, click and drag to resize the chart.

Alternatively, after clicking the chart's border, you can use the Format ➪ Size controls for more precise adjustments to the height and width of the chart. Simply select or type the dimensions directly into the Height and Width controls.

To move an embedded chart, just click its border at any location except one of the eight resizing handles. Then drag the chart to its new location. You also can use standard cut-and-paste techniques to move an embedded chart. Select the chart and choose Home ⇨ Clipboard ⇨ Cut (or press Ctrl+X). Then activate a cell near the desired location and choose Home ⇨ Clipboard ⇨ Paste (or press Ctrl+V).

The new location can be in a different worksheet or even in a different workbook. If you paste the chart to a different workbook, it will be linked to the data in the original workbook. Another way to move a chart to a different location is to choose Chart Design ⇨ Location ⇨ Move Chart. This command displays the Move Chart dialog box, which lets you specify a new sheet for the chart (either a chart sheet or a worksheet).

Converting an Embedded Chart to a Chart Sheet

When you create a chart using the icons in the Insert ⇨ Charts group, the result is always an embedded chart. If you'd prefer that your chart be located on a chart sheet, you can easily move it.

To convert an embedded chart to a chart on a chart sheet, select the chart and choose Chart Design ⇨ Location ⇨ Move Chart to display the Move Chart dialog box shown in Figure 11.15. Select the New Sheet option and (optionally) provide a different name for the chart sheet.

FIGURE 11.15

Use the Move Chart dialog box to move an embedded chart to a chart sheet (or vice versa).

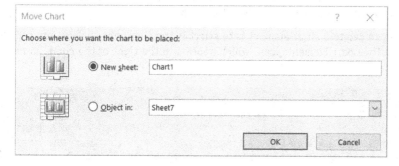

To convert a chart on a chart sheet to an embedded chart, activate the chart sheet and then choose Chart Design ⇨ Location ⇨ Move Chart to display the Move Chart dialog box. Select the Object In option and specify the sheet by using the drop-down list.

Copying a Chart

To make an exact copy of an embedded chart, select the chart and choose Home ⇨ Clipboard ⇨ Copy (or press Ctrl+C). Then activate a cell near the desired location and choose Home ⇨ Clipboard ⇨ Paste (or press Ctrl+V). The new location can be in a different worksheet or even in a different workbook. If you paste the chart to a different workbook, it will be linked to the data in the original workbook.

To copy a chart on a chart sheet, press Ctrl while you drag the sheet tab to a new location in the tab list.

Deleting a Chart

To delete an embedded chart, simply click the chart and then press Delete. When the Ctrl key is pressed, you can select multiple charts and then delete them all with a single press of the Delete key.

To delete a chart sheet, right-click its sheet tab and choose Delete from the context menu. To delete multiple chart sheets, select them by pressing Ctrl while you click the sheet tabs.

Adding Chart Elements

To add new elements to a chart (such as a title, legend, data labels, or gridlines), activate the chart and use the controls in the Chart Elements + icon, which appears to the right of the chart. Note that each item expands to display additional options.

You can also use Add Chart Element on the Chart Design tab, in the Chart Layouts group.

Moving and Deleting Chart Elements

Some elements within a chart can be moved: titles, legend, and data labels. To move a chart element, simply click it to select it and then drag its border.

The easiest way to delete a chart element is to select it and then press Delete. You can also use the controls on the Chart Elements icon, which appears to the right of the chart, to reposition chart elements.

> **NOTE**
>
> A few chart elements consist of multiple objects. For example, the data labels element consists of one label for each data point. To move or delete one data label, click once to select the entire element and then click a second time to select the specific data label. You can then move or delete the single data label.

Formatting Chart Elements

Many users are content to stick with the predefined chart styles and layouts. For more precise customizations, Excel allows you to work with individual chart elements and apply additional formatting. You can use the Ribbon commands for some modifications, but the easiest way to format chart elements is to right-click the element and choose Format <Element> from the context menu. The exact command depends on the element that you select. For example, if you right-click the chart's title, the context menu command is Format Chart Title.

The Format command displays a task pane with options for the selected element. Changes that you make are displayed immediately in the chart. When you select a new chart element, the task pane changes to display the properties for the newly selected element. You can keep this task pane displayed while you work on the chart. It can be docked alongside the left or right part of the window or made free-floating and sizable.

> **TIP**
> If the Format task pane isn't displayed, you can double-click a chart element to display it.

Refer to the sidebar "Exploring the Format Task Pane" for an explanation of how the Format task panes work.

> **TIP**
> If you apply formatting to a chart element and decide that it wasn't such a good idea, you can revert to the original formatting for the particular chart style. Right-click the chart element and choose Reset to Match Style from the context menu. To reset the entire chart, select the chart area when you issue the command.

Exploring the Format Task Pane

The Format task pane can be a bit deceiving. It contains many options that aren't visible, and you sometimes have to do quite a bit of clicking to find the formatting option you want.

The name of a given Format task pane depends on which chart element is selected. For instance, Figure 11.14 shows the task pane for a data series. The options available on the Format task pane will vary quite a bit, depending on which chart element you selected.

Regardless of the element that you select, however, the Format task pane will present you with icons at the top. Each icon has its own set of controls, which can be expanded to expose a set of formatting and customization options.

At first, the Format task pane will seem complicated and confusing. But as you get better acquainted with it, using the task pane gets much easier.

Copying a Chart's Formatting

If you create a nicely formatted chart and realize that you need to create several more charts that have the same formatting, you have these three choices:

- **Make a copy of the original chart and then change the data used in the copied chart:** One way to change the data used in a chart is to choose the Chart Design ➪ Data ➪ Select Data command and make the changes in the Select Data Source dialog box.

- **Create the other charts, but don't apply any formatting:** Then activate the original chart and press Ctrl+C. Select one of the other charts, and choose Home ⇨ Clipboard ⇨ Paste ⇨ Paste Special. In the Paste Special dialog box, click the Formats option and then click OK. Repeat for each additional chart.
- **Create a chart template and then use the template as the basis for the new charts, or you can apply the new template to existing charts.**

> **NOTE**
>
> To create a chart template, right-click the chart and click Save as Template. Type a name for the chart in the File Name text box of the Save Chart Template dialog box, and then click Save. Excel saves chart templates in the Templates folder of the All Charts tab in the Insert Chart and Change Chart Types dialog boxes.

Renaming a Chart

When you activate an embedded chart, its name appears in the Name box (located to the left of the Formula bar). To change the name of an embedded chart, simply select the chart and then enter the desired name in the Name box.

Why rename a chart? If a worksheet has many charts, you may prefer to activate a particular chart by name. Just type the chart's name in the Name box and press Enter. It's much easier to remember a chart named Monthly Sales as opposed to a chart named Chart9.

> **NOTE**
>
> When you rename a chart, Excel allows you to use a name that already exists for another chart. Normally, it doesn't matter if multiple charts have the same name, but it can cause problems if you use Visual Basic for Applications (VBA) macros that select a chart by name.

Printing Charts

Printing embedded charts is nothing special; you print them the same way that you print a worksheet. As long as you include the embedded chart in the range that you want to print, Excel prints the chart as it appears onscreen. When printing a sheet that contains embedded charts, it's a good idea to preview first (or use Page Layout view) to ensure that your charts don't span multiple pages. If you created the chart on a chart sheet, Excel always prints the chart on a page by itself.

> **TIP**
>
> If you select an embedded chart and choose File ⇨ Print, Excel prints the chart on a page by itself and does *not* print the worksheet data.

If you don't want a particular embedded chart to appear on your printout, access the Format Chart Area task pane and click the Size & Properties icon. Then expand the Properties section and deselect the Print Object option.

Understanding Chart Types

IN THIS CHAPTER

- Reviewing available chart types and when to use them
- Exploring newer special purpose chart types

With the wide variety of chart types and chart subtypes available in Excel, sometimes it can become difficult to identify which type of chart will best present your data. This chapter walks you through available chart types so you can have more confidence selecting the right chart type to present your data.

 The sample workbook for this chapter (`Intro to Charts.xlsx`) can be found at www.wiley .com/go/excelquickandeasy.

Choosing a Chart Type

People who create charts usually do so to make a point or to communicate a specific message. Often, the message is explicitly stated in the chart's title or in a text box within the chart. The chart itself provides visual support.

Choosing the correct chart type is often a key factor in the effectiveness of the message. Therefore, it's often well worth your time to experiment with various chart types to determine which one conveys your message best.

In almost every case, the underlying message in a chart is some type of comparison. Examples of some general types of comparisons include the following:

- **Comparing an item to other items:** A chart may compare sales in each of a company's sales regions.
- **Comparing data over time:** A chart may display sales by month and indicate trends over time.
- **Making relative comparisons:** A common pie chart can depict relative proportions in terms of pie "slices."
- **Comparing data relationships:** An XY chart is ideal for this comparison. For example, you might show the relationship between monthly marketing expenditures and sales.

- **Comparing frequency:** You can use a common histogram, for example, to display the number (or percentage) of students who scored within a particular grade range.
- **Identifying outliers or unusual situations:** If you have thousands of data points, creating a chart may help identify data that isn't representative.

A common question among Excel users is "How do I know which chart type to use for my data?" Unfortunately, this question has no cut-and-dried answer. Perhaps the best answer is a vague one: Use the chart type that gets your message across in the simplest way. A good starting point is Excel's recommended charts. Select your data and choose Insert ➪ Charts ➪ Recommended Charts to see the chart types that Excel suggests. Remember that these suggestions are not always the best choices.

> **NOTE**
>
> In the Ribbon, the Charts group of the Insert tab shows the Recommended Charts button, plus nine other drop-down buttons. All of these drop-down buttons display multiple chart types. For example, column and bar charts are all available from a single drop-down button. Similarly, scatter charts and bubble charts share a single button. Probably the easiest way to choose a particular chart type is to select Insert ➪ Charts ➪ Recommended Charts, which displays the Insert Chart dialog box with the Recommended Charts tab displayed. Select the All Charts tab, and you'll have a concise list of all chart and subchart types.

Figure 12.1 shows the same set of data plotted by using six different chart types. Although all six charts represent the same information (monthly website visitors), they look quite different from one another.

The column chart (upper left) is probably the best choice for this particular set of data because it clearly shows the information for each month in discrete units. The bar chart (upper right) is similar to a column chart, but since the axes are swapped and most people are more accustomed to seeing time-based information extend from left to right rather than from top to bottom, this isn't the optimal choice.

The line chart (middle left) may not be the best choice because it can imply that the data is continuous—that points exist in between the 12 actual data points. This same argument may be made against using an area chart (middle right).

The pie chart (lower left) is simply too confusing and does nothing to convey the time-based nature of the data. Pie charts are most appropriate for a data series in which you want to emphasize proportions among a relatively small number of data points. If you have too many data points, a pie chart can be impossible to interpret.

The radar chart (lower right) is clearly inappropriate for this data. People aren't accustomed to viewing time-based information in a circular direction!

Fortunately, changing a chart's type is easy, so you can experiment with various chart types until you find the one that represents your data accurately, clearly, and as simply as possible.

FIGURE 12.1

The same data, plotted by using six chart types

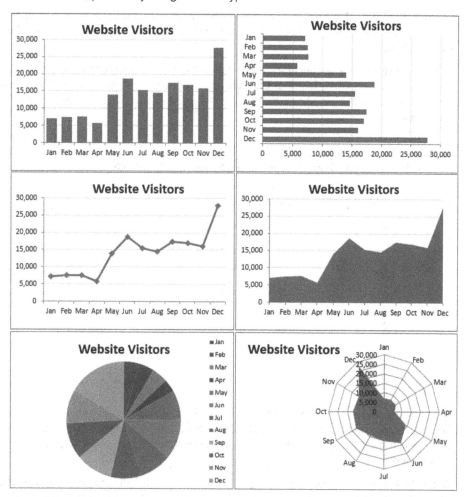

The remainder of this chapter contains more information about the various Excel chart types. The examples and discussion may give you a better handle on determining the most appropriate chart type for your data.

Column Charts

Probably the most common chart type is the *column chart*, which displays each data point as a vertical column, the height of which corresponds to the value. The value scale is displayed on the vertical axis, which is usually on the left side of the chart. You can specify any number of data series, and the corresponding data points from each series can be stacked on top of each other. Typically, each data series is depicted in a different color or pattern.

Column charts are often used to compare discrete items, and they can depict the differences between items in a series or items across multiple series. Excel offers seven column-chart subtypes.

Figure 12.2 shows an example of a clustered column chart that depicts monthly sales for two products. From this chart, it's clear that Sprocket sales have always exceeded Widget sales. In addition, Widget sales have been declining over the five-month period, whereas Sprocket sales are increasing.

FIGURE 12.2

This clustered column chart compares monthly sales for two products.

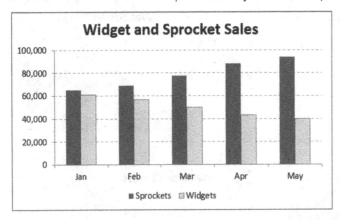

The same data, in the form of a stacked column chart, is shown in Figure 12.3. This chart has the added advantage of depicting the combined sales over time. It shows that total sales have remained fairly steady each month, but the relative proportions of the two products have changed.

Figure 12.4 shows the same sales data plotted as a 100% stacked column chart. This chart type shows the relative contribution of each product by month. Notice that the vertical axis displays percentage values, not sales amounts. This chart provides no information about the actual sales volumes, but such information could be provided using data labels. This type of chart is often a good alternative to using several pie charts. Instead of using a pie to show the relative sales volume in each year, the chart uses a column for each year.

Figure 12.5 shows the same data plotted with a 3D clustered column chart. Many people use this type of chart to add some visual pizzazz, but it's generally considered bad practice to use 3D charts because precise comparisons are difficult due to the distorted perspective view.

FIGURE 12.3

This stacked column chart displays sales by product and depicts the total sales.

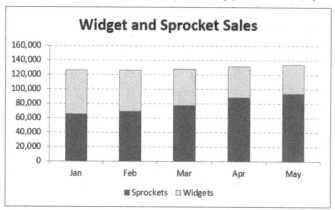

FIGURE 12.4

This 100% stacked column chart displays monthly sales as a percentage.

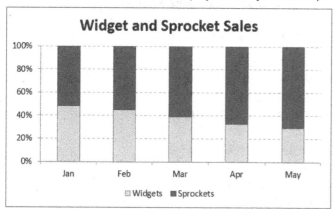

Bar Charts

A *bar chart* is essentially a column chart that has been rotated 90 degrees clockwise. One distinct advantage to using a bar chart is that the category labels may be easier to read. Figure 12.6 shows a bar chart that displays a value for each of 10 survey items. The category labels are lengthy, and displaying them legibly with a column chart would be difficult. Excel offers six bar chart subtypes.

You can include any number of data series in a bar chart. In addition, the bars can be "stacked" from left to right.

FIGURE 12.5

A 3D column chart

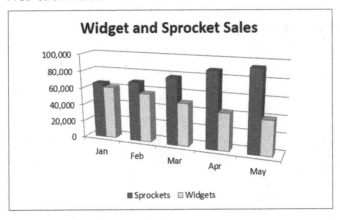

FIGURE 12.6

If you have lengthy category labels, a bar chart may be a good choice.

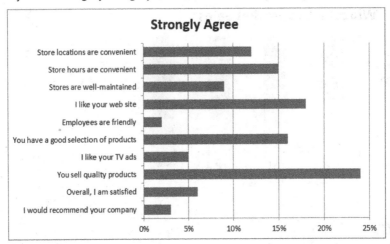

Line Charts

Line charts are often used to plot continuous data and are useful for identifying trends. For example, plotting daily sales as a line chart may enable you to identify sales fluctuations over time. Normally, the category axis for a line chart displays equal intervals. Excel supports seven line chart subtypes.

See Figure 12.7 for an example of a line chart that depicts monthly data (675 data points). Although the data varies quite a bit monthly, the chart clearly depicts the cycles.

FIGURE 12.7

A line chart often can help you spot trends in your data.

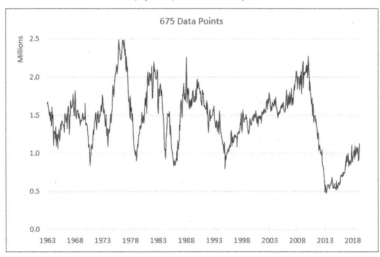

A line chart can use any number of data series, and you distinguish the lines by using different colors, line styles, or markers. Figure 12.8 shows a line chart that has three series. The series are distinguished by markers (circles, squares, and triangles) and different line colors. When the chart is printed in black and white, the markers are the only way to identify the lines.

FIGURE 12.8

This line chart displays three series.

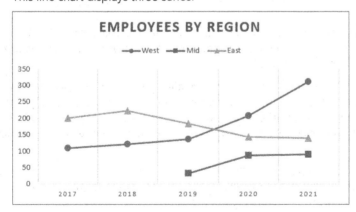

The final line chart example, shown in Figure 12.9, is a 3D line chart. Although it has a nice visual appeal, it's certainly not the clearest way to present the data. In fact, it's fairly worthless.

FIGURE 12.9

This 3D line chart does not present the data very well.

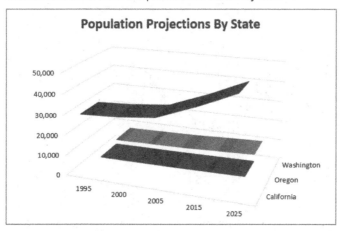

Pie Charts

A *pie chart* is useful when you want to show relative proportions or contributions to a whole. A pie chart uses only one data series. Pie charts are most effective with a small number of data points. Generally, a pie chart should use no more than five or six data points (or slices). A pie chart with too many data points can be difficult to interpret.

> **CAUTION**
>
> All of the values in a pie chart must be positive numbers. If you create a pie chart that uses one or more negative values, the negative values will be converted to positive values, which is probably not what you intended.

You can "explode" one or more slices of a pie chart for emphasis (see Figure 12.10). Activate the chart and click any pie slice to select the entire pie. Then click the slice that you want to explode and drag it away from the center.

The "pie of pie" and "bar of pie" chart subtypes enable you to display a secondary chart that provides more detail for one of the pie slices. Figure 12.11 shows an example of a bar of pie chart. The pie chart shows the breakdown of four expense categories: Rent, Supplies, Utilities, and Salary. The secondary bar chart provides an additional regional breakdown of the Salary category.

The data used in the chart resides in A2:B8. When the chart was created, Excel made a guess as to which categories belong to the secondary chart. In this case, the guess was to use the last three data points for the secondary chart—and the guess was incorrect.

FIGURE 12.10

A pie chart with one slice exploded

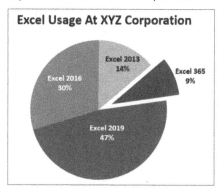

FIGURE 12.11

A bar of pie chart that shows detail for one of the pie slices

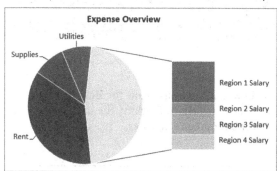

To correct the chart, right-click any of the pie slices and choose Format Data Series. In the Format Data Series task pane, select the Series Options icon and make the changes. In this example, we chose Split Series By Position and specified that the second plot contains four values in the series.

Another pie chart subtype is called a *doughnut chart*. It's basically a pie chart with a hole in the middle. Unlike a pie chart, however, a doughnut chart can display multiple series.

XY (Scatter) Charts

Another common chart type is an *XY chart* (also known as *scatter grams* or *scatter plots*). An XY chart differs from most other chart types in that both axes display values. (An XY chart has no category axis.)

This type of chart often is used to show the relationship between two variables. Figure 12.12 shows an example of an XY chart that plots the relationship between weeks in a weight loss program (horizontal axis) and weight lost (vertical axis).

FIGURE 12.12

An XY chart shows the relationship between two variables.

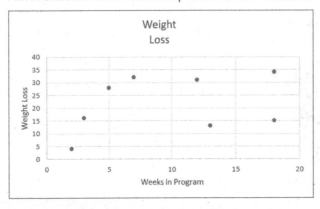

NOTE

Although these data points correspond to time, the chart doesn't convey any time-related information. In other words, the data points are plotted based only on their two values.

Area Charts

Think of an *area chart* as a line chart in which the areas below the lines have been filled. Figure 12.13 shows an example of a stacked area chart. Stacking the data series enables you to see the total clearly, as well as the contribution by each series.

FIGURE 12.13

A stacked area chart

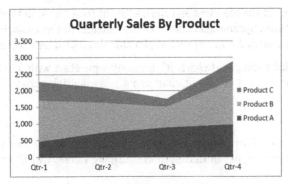

Figure 12.14 shows the same data, plotted as a 3D area chart. As you can see, it's not an example of an effective chart. The data for products B and C is partially obscured. In some cases,

the problem can be resolved by rotating the chart or using transparency. But usually the best way to salvage a chart like this is to select a new chart type.

FIGURE 12.14

This 3D area chart is not a good choice.

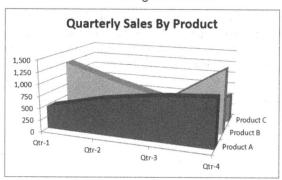

Radar Charts

You may not be familiar with this type of chart. A *radar chart* is a specialized chart that has a separate axis for each category, and the axes extend outward from the center of the chart. The value of each data point is plotted on the corresponding axis.

Figure 12.15 shows an example of a radar chart on the left. This chart plots two data series across 12 categories (months) and shows the seasonal demand for snow skis versus water skis. Note that the water-ski series partially obscures the snow-ski series.

FIGURE 12.15

Plotting ski sales using a radar chart with 12 categories and two series

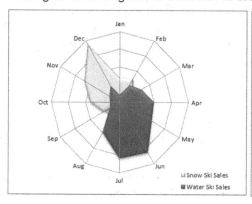

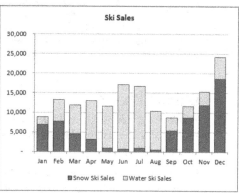

Using a radar chart to show seasonal sales may be an interesting approach, but it's certainly not the best chart type. As you can see, the stacked bar chart on the right shows the information much more clearly.

Surface Charts

Surface charts display two or more data series on a surface. As Figure 12.16 shows, these charts can be quite interesting. Unlike other charts, Excel uses color to distinguish values, not to distinguish the data series. The number of colors used is determined by the major unit scale setting for the value axis. Each color corresponds to one major unit.

FIGURE 12.16

A surface chart

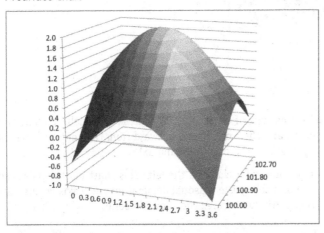

> **NOTE**
>
> A surface chart does not plot 3D data points. The series axis for a surface chart, as with all other 3D charts, is a category axis—not a value axis. In other words, if you have data that is represented by x, y, and z coordinates, it can't be plotted accurately on a surface chart unless the x and y values are equally spaced.

Bubble Charts

Think of a *bubble chart* as an XY chart that can display an additional data series, which is represented by the size of the bubbles. As with an XY chart, both axes are value axes. (There is no category axis.)

Figure 12.17 shows an example of a bubble chart that depicts the results of a weight-loss program. The horizontal value axis represents the original weight, the vertical value axis shows the number of weeks in the program, and the size of the bubbles represents the amount of weight lost.

FIGURE 12.17

A bubble chart

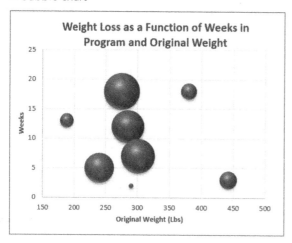

12

Stock Charts

Stock charts are most useful for displaying stock-market information. These charts require three to five data series, depending on the subtype.

Figure 12.18 shows an example of each of the four stock chart types. The two charts on the bottom display the trade volume and use two value axes. The daily volume, represented by columns, uses the axis on the left. The *up-bars*, sometimes referred to as *candlesticks*, are the vertical lines that depict the difference between the opening and closing price. A black up-bar indicates that the closing price was lower than the opening price.

Stock charts aren't just for stock price data. Figure 12.19 shows a stock chart that depicts the high, low, and average temperatures for each day in May. This is a high-low-close chart.

Newer Chart Types for Excel

This section presents examples of more modern advanced chart types along with an explanation of the type of data required.

Histogram Charts

Histogram charts display the count of data items in each of several discrete bins. Those of us who have used the Analysis ToolPak in the past to create histogram charts will tell you that it took some effort to create a nice-looking chart. However, the new histogram chart type makes short work of the task.

FIGURE 12.18

The four stock chart subtypes

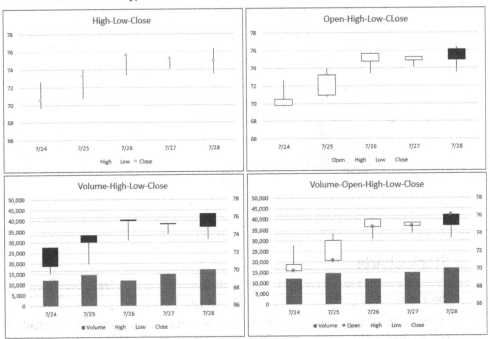

FIGURE 12.19

Plotting temperature data with a stock chart

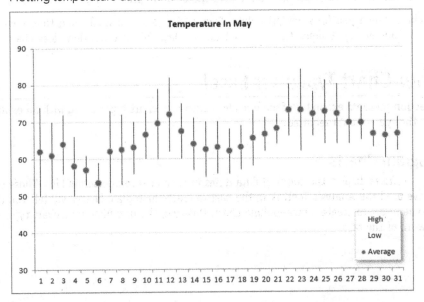

Figure 12.20 shows a histogram created from 105 student test scores. The bins are displayed as category labels. You control the number of bins by using the **Axis Options** section of the Format Axis task pane. In this example, we specified eight bins, and Excel took care of all of the details.

FIGURE 12.20

Displaying a student grade distribution using a histogram chart

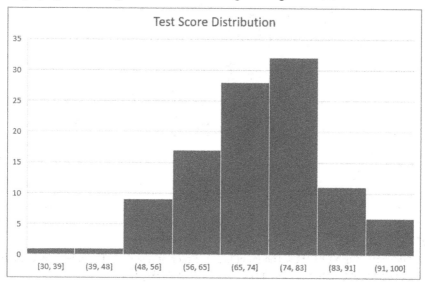

Pareto Charts

The *Pareto chart* type is a combination chart in which columns are displayed in descending order, and the columns use the left axis. The line shows the cumulative percentage and uses the right axis.

Figure 12.21 shows a Pareto chart created from the data in the range A2:B14. Notice that Excel sorted the items in the chart. The line shows, for example, that approximately 50% of all complaints are in the top three categories.

> **NOTE**
> The Pareto chart type is actually a Histogram subtype. You can find the Pareto chart type under Insert ⮑ Charts ⮑ Insert Statistic Chart.

FIGURE 12.21

A Pareto chart displays the number of complaints graphically.

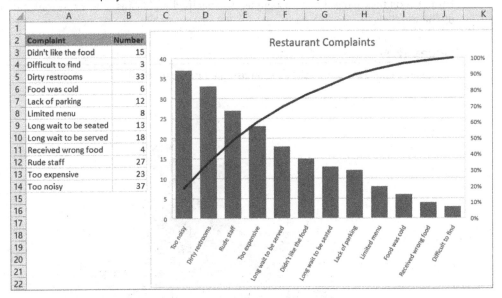

Waterfall Charts

A *waterfall chart* is used to show the cumulative effect of a series of numbers, usually both positive and negative numbers. The result is a staircase-like display.

Figure 12.22 shows a waterfall chart that uses the data in column D. Waterfall charts typically display the ending total as the last bar, with its origin at zero. To display the total column correctly, select the column, right-click, and choose Set As Total from the context menu.

Box & Whisker Charts

A *box & whisker chart* is often used to summarize data visually. In the past, it was possible to create such charts using Excel, but it required quite a bit of setup work. Now, it's simple.

Figure 12.23 shows a box & whisker chart created for four groups of subjects. The data is in a two-column table. In the chart, the vertical lines extending from the box represent the numerical range of the data (minimum and maximum values). The "boxes" represent the 25th through the 75th percentile. The horizontal line inside the box is the median value (or 50th percentile), and the X is the average. This type of chart enables the viewer to make quick comparisons among groups of data.

The Series Options section of the Format Data Series task pane contains some options for this chart type.

FIGURE 12.22

A waterfall chart showing positive and negative net cash flows

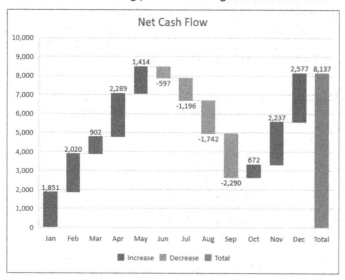

FIGURE 12.23

A box & whisker chart that summarizes data for four groups

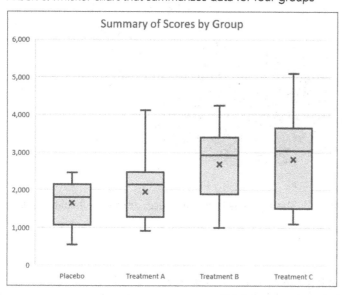

Sunburst Charts

Sunburst charts are like pie charts with multiple concentric layers. This chart type is most useful for data that's organized hierarchically. Figure 12.24 shows an example of a sunburst chart that depicts a music collection. It shows the number of tracks by genre and subgenre. For example, you'll see in Figure 12.24 that jazz is a genre of music, and within that genre, there are vocal and instrumental subgenres. Also note that some genres have no subgenres.

FIGURE 12.24

A sunburst chart that depicts a music collection by genre and subgenre

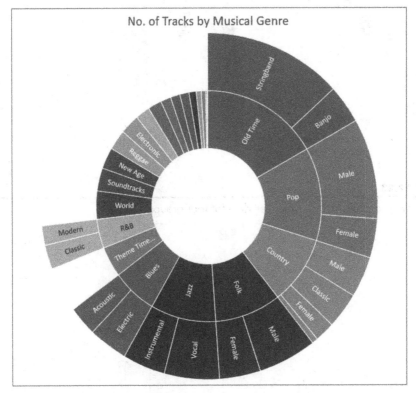

A potential problem with this chart type is that some slices are so small that the data labels can't be displayed.

Treemap Charts

Like a sunburst chart, a treemap chart is suited for hierarchical data. The data, however, is represented as rectangles. Figure 12.25 shows the data from the previous example, plotted as a treemap chart.

FIGURE 12.25

A treemap chart that depicts a music collection by genre and subgenre

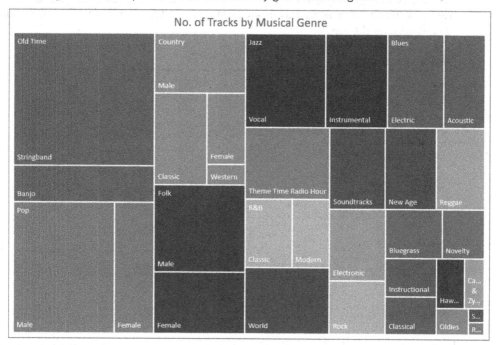

Funnel Charts

Funnel charts are ideal for representing the relative values in each stage of a process. These charts are typically used to visualize sales pipelines (see Figure 12.26).

FIGURE 12.26

A funnel chart visualizing the value in each stage of a sales pipeline

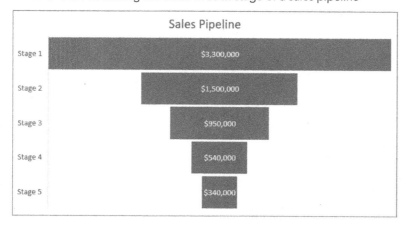

Map Charts

Map charts leverage Bing maps to render location-based visualizations. As you can see in Figure 12.27, all you need to provide are location indicators (in this case, country names), and then Excel does the rest.

FIGURE 12.27

Map charts are ideal for visualizing location-based data.

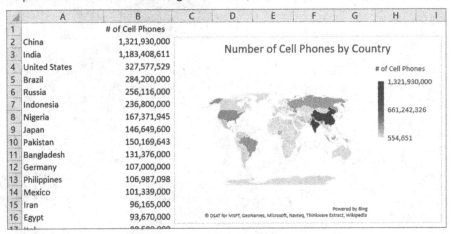

Map charts are remarkably flexible, allowing you create a chart based on province names, county names, cities, and even ZIP codes. As long as Bing can recognize the values that you are using to identify geography, your chart will render seamlessly.

Double-clicking the map will activate the Format Data Series task pane (see Figure 12.28), exposing a handful of unique formatting options. These options allow you to change the projection (flat or curved map), the area (show all locations or just those that have data), and the series color (apply color banding based on values).

FIGURE 12.28

Map charts come with unique customization options.

Printing Your Work

IN THIS CHAPTER

- Changing your worksheet view
- Adjusting your print settings for better results
- Adding a header or footer to a printout

Despite predictions of the "paperless office," paper remains an excellent way to carry information around and share it with others, particularly if there's no electricity or Wi-Fi where you're going. Some of the worksheets that you develop with Excel will end up as hard-copy reports, and you'll want them to look as good as possible. You'll find that printing from Excel is quite easy and that you can generate attractive, well-formatted reports with minimal effort. In addition, Excel has many options that give you a great deal of control over the printed page. We explain these options in this chapter.

Doing Basic Printing

If you want to print a copy of a worksheet with no fuss and bother, use the Quick Print option. One way to access this command is to choose File ⇨ Print (which displays the Print pane of Backstage view) and then click the Print button. The keyboard shortcut Ctrl+P has the same effect as File ⇨ Print. When you use Ctrl+P to show Backstage view, the Print button has the focus, so you can simply press Enter to print.

If you like the idea of one-click printing, take a few seconds to add a new button to your Quick Access Toolbar. Click the down-pointing arrow on the right of the Quick Access Toolbar and then choose Quick Print from the drop-down list. Excel adds the Quick Print icon to your Quick Access Toolbar.

Clicking the Quick Print button prints the current worksheet on the currently selected printer, using the default print settings. If you've changed any of the default print settings (by using the Page Layout tab), Excel uses the new settings; otherwise, it uses the following default settings:

- Prints the active worksheet (or all selected worksheets), including any embedded charts or objects
- Prints one copy
- Prints the entire active worksheet

- Prints in portrait mode
- Doesn't scale the printed output
- Uses letter-size paper with 0.75-inch margins for the top and bottom and 0.70-inch margins for the left and right margins
- Prints with no headers or footers
- Doesn't print cell notes or comments
- Prints with no cell gridlines
- For wide worksheets that span multiple pages, prints down and then over

When you print a worksheet, Excel prints only the active area of the worksheet. In other words, it won't print all 17 billion cells—just those that have data in them. If the worksheet contains any embedded charts or other graphic objects (such as SmartArt or shapes), they're also printed.

Using Print Preview

When you choose File ⇨ Print (or press Ctrl+P), Backstage view displays a preview of your printed output, exactly as it will be printed. Initially, Excel displays the first page of your printed output. To view subsequent pages, use the page controls along the bottom of the preview pane (or use the vertical scrollbar along the right side of the screen).

The Print Preview window has a few other commands (at the bottom) that you can use while previewing your output. For a multipage printout, use the page number controls to jump quickly to a particular page. The Show Margins button toggles the display of margins, and Zoom To Page ensures that a complete page is displayed.

When the Show Margins option is enabled, Excel adds markers to the preview that indicate column borders and margins. You can drag the column or margin markers to make changes that appear onscreen. Changes that you make to column widths in preview mode are also made in the actual worksheet.

Print Preview is certainly useful, but you may prefer to use Page Layout view to preview your output (see the next section, "Changing Your Page View").

Changing Your Page View

Page Layout view shows your worksheet divided into pages. In other words, you can visualize your printed output while you work.

Page Layout view is one of three worksheet views, which are controlled by the three icons on the right side of the status bar. You could also use the commands in the View ⇨ Workbook Views group on the Ribbon to switch views. The three view options are as follows:

- **Normal:** The default view of the worksheet. This view may or may not show page breaks.

- **Page Layout:** Shows individual pages.
- **Page Break Preview:** Allows you to adjust page breaks manually.

Just click one of the icons to change the view. You can also use the Zoom slider to change the magnification from 10% (a very tiny, bird's-eye view) to 400% (very large, for showing fine detail).

The following sections describe how these views can help with printing.

Normal View

Most of the time when you work in Excel, you use Normal view. Normal view can display page breaks in the worksheet. The page breaks are indicated by horizontal and vertical dotted lines. These page break lines adjust automatically if you change the page orientation, insert or delete rows or columns, change row heights, change column widths, and so on. For example, if you find that your printed output is too wide to fit on a single page, you can adjust the column widths (keeping an eye on the page break display) until the columns are narrow enough to print on one page.

NOTE

Page breaks aren't displayed until you print (or preview) the worksheet at least one time. Page breaks are also displayed if you set a print area by choosing Page Layout ➪ Page Setup ➪ Print Area.

TIP

If you'd prefer not to see the page break in Normal view, choose File ➪ Options and select the Advanced tab. Scroll down to the Display Options For This Worksheet section and deselect Show Page Breaks. This setting applies only to the active worksheet and is grayed out if you're in anything but Normal view. Unfortunately, the option to turn off page break display is not on the Ribbon, and it's not even available for inclusion on the Quick Access Toolbar.

Figure 13.1 shows a part of a worksheet in Normal view with gridlines turned off. You can see the dotted line between columns D and E that indicates a page break.

Page Layout View

Unlike the preview in Backstage view (choose File ➪ Print), Page Layout view is not a view-only mode. You have complete access to all Excel commands. In fact, you can use Page Layout view all the time if you like.

Figure 13.2 shows a worksheet in Page Layout view, zoomed to about 40% to show multiple pages. Contrary to Normal view, you can see the margins, the page header and footer (if any), and even some space separating each page. If you've specified any repeated rows and columns, they are also displayed—giving you a true preview of the printed output.

13

FIGURE 13.1

In Normal view, dotted lines indicate page breaks.

	A	B	C	D	E
1	Noah	Mcdonald	Colonial Movers	Bridgeport	Mississippi
2	Elijah	Daniels	LexCorp	Hialeah	Maryland
3	Chase	Ruiz	Roxxon	Portland	California
4	Jonathan	Ward	Charles Townsend Agency	Wichita	Illinois
5	Jacob	Cole	Minuteman Cafe	El Paso	New Jersey
6	Abigail	Martin	United Fried Chicken	Amarillo	South Dakota
7	Allison	Simpson	Universal Export	Daly City	Mississippi
8	Elizabeth	Coleman	Input, Inc.	Springfield	Florida
9	Arianna	Greene	Wayne Enterprises	Ontario	Texas
10	James	Lewis	Spacely Sprockets	Green Bay	Kentucky
11	Jack	Andrews	Gringotts	Pittsburgh	Iowa
12	Sofia	Freeman	Krustyco	Spokane	Oregon
13	Ayden	Gray	Keedsler Motors	San Bernardino	Georgia
14	Adam	King	The Frying Dutchman	St. Petersburg	Michigan
15	Gavin	Alexander	Galaxy Corp	Rancho Cucamonga	Hawaii
16	Leah	Turner	Extensive Enterprise	Long Beach	Tennessee
17	Gianna	Peters	Dunder Mifflin	Garden Grove	New Hampshire
18	Sophia	Hall	Spade and Archer	Gresham	Kentucky
19	Ryan	Davis	The Krusty Krab	Salem	Louisiana
20	Brooke	Gray	Wentworth Industries	Erie	South Dakota
21	Tristan	West	Wayne Enterprises	Elk Grove	Nevada
22	Dominic	Andrews	The Legitimate Businessmens Club	Oxnard	Utah
23	Kaden	Woods	Sample, inc	Coral Springs	Missouri

TIP

If you move the mouse to the corner of a page while in Page Layout view, you can click to hide the whitespace in the margins. Doing so gives you all the advantages of Page Layout view, but you can see more information onscreen because the unused margin space is hidden.

Page Break Preview

Page Break Preview displays the worksheet and the page breaks. Figure 13.3 shows an example. This view mode is different from Normal view mode with page breaks turned on. The key difference is that you can drag the page breaks. You can also drag the edges of the print area to change its size (if you've set a print area). Unlike Page Layout view, Page Break Preview does not display margins, headers, or footers.

When you enter Page Break Preview, Excel performs the following:

- Changes the zoom factor so that you can see more of the worksheet
- Displays the page numbers overlaid on the pages
- Displays the current print range with a white background; nonprinting areas appear with a gray background
- Displays all page breaks as draggable dashed lines

FIGURE 13.2

In Page Layout view, the worksheet resembles printed pages.

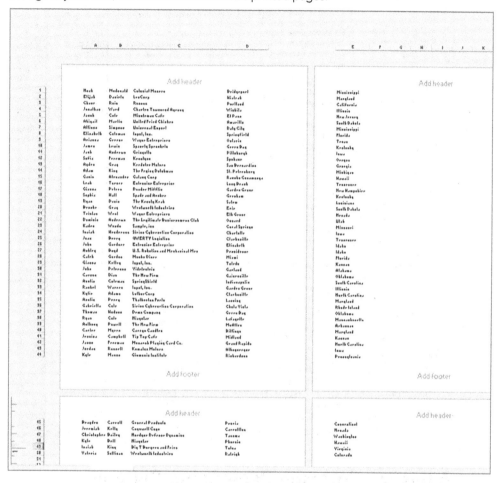

13

When you change the page breaks by dragging, Excel automatically adjusts the scaling so that the information fits on the pages, per your specifications.

TIP

In Page Break Preview, you still have access to all Excel commands. You can change the zoom factor if you find the text to be too small.

To exit Page Break Preview, just click one of the other View icons on the right side of the status bar.

FIGURE 13.3

Page Break Preview allows you to drag page breaks and print area borders.

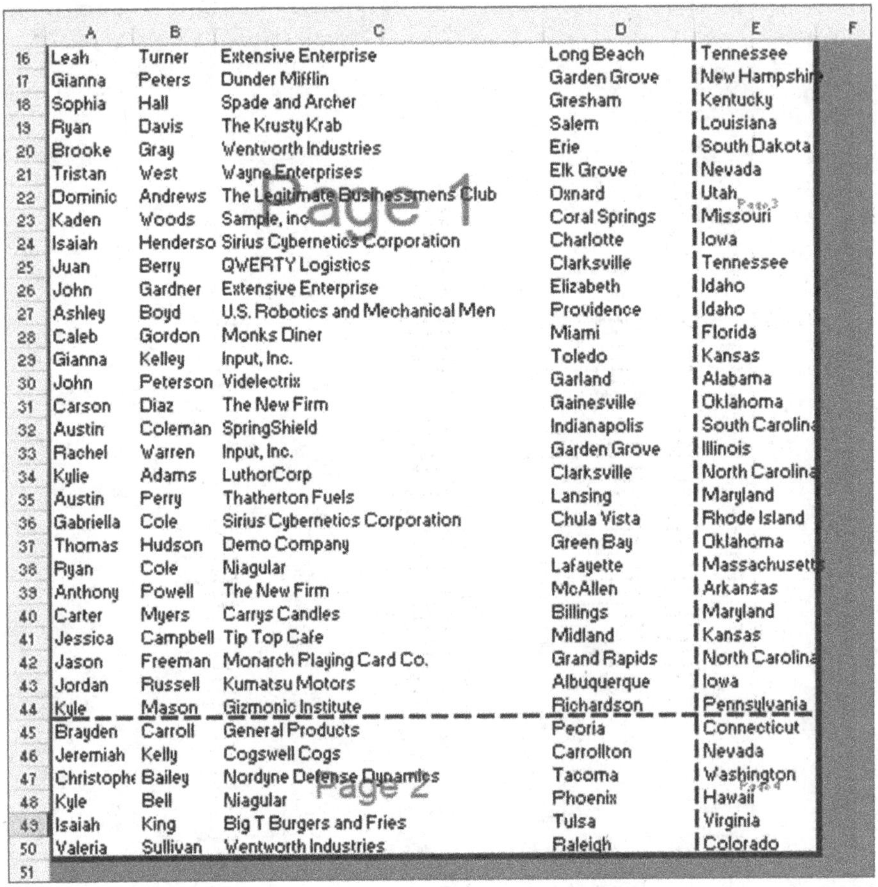

	A	B	C	D	E	F
16	Leah	Turner	Extensive Enterprise	Long Beach	Tennessee	
17	Gianna	Peters	Dunder Mifflin	Garden Grove	New Hampshire	
18	Sophia	Hall	Spade and Archer	Gresham	Kentucky	
19	Ryan	Davis	The Krusty Krab	Salem	Louisiana	
20	Brooke	Gray	Wentworth Industries	Erie	South Dakota	
21	Tristan	West	Wayne Enterprises	Elk Grove	Nevada	
22	Dominic	Andrews	The Legitimate Businessmens Club	Oxnard	Utah	
23	Kaden	Woods	Sample, inc	Coral Springs	Missouri	
24	Isaiah	Henderso	Sirius Cybernetics Corporation	Charlotte	Iowa	
25	Juan	Berry	QWERTY Logistics	Clarksville	Tennessee	
26	John	Gardner	Extensive Enterprise	Elizabeth	Idaho	
27	Ashley	Boyd	U.S. Robotics and Mechanical Men	Providence	Idaho	
28	Caleb	Gordon	Monks Diner	Miami	Florida	
29	Gianna	Kelley	Input, Inc.	Toledo	Kansas	
30	John	Peterson	Videlectrix	Garland	Alabama	
31	Carson	Diaz	The New Firm	Gainesville	Oklahoma	
32	Austin	Coleman	SpringShield	Indianapolis	South Carolina	
33	Rachel	Warren	Input, Inc.	Garden Grove	Illinois	
34	Kylie	Adams	LuthorCorp	Clarksville	North Carolina	
35	Austin	Perry	Thatherton Fuels	Lansing	Maryland	
36	Gabriella	Cole	Sirius Cybernetics Corporation	Chula Vista	Rhode Island	
37	Thomas	Hudson	Demo Company	Green Bay	Oklahoma	
38	Ryan	Cole	Niagular	Lafayette	Massachusetts	
39	Anthony	Powell	The New Firm	McAllen	Arkansas	
40	Carter	Myers	Carrys Candles	Billings	Maryland	
41	Jessica	Campbell	Tip Top Cafe	Midland	Kansas	
42	Jason	Freeman	Monarch Playing Card Co.	Grand Rapids	North Carolina	
43	Jordan	Russell	Kumatsu Motors	Albuquerque	Iowa	
44	Kyle	Mason	Gizmonic Institute	Richardson	Pennsylvania	
45	Brayden	Carroll	General Products	Peoria	Connecticut	
46	Jeremiah	Kelly	Cogswell Cogs	Carrollton	Nevada	
47	Christophe	Bailey	Nordyne Defense Dynamics	Tacoma	Washington	
48	Kyle	Bell	Niagular	Phoenix	Hawaii	
49	Isaiah	King	Big T Burgers and Fries	Tulsa	Virginia	
50	Valeria	Sullivan	Wentworth Industries	Raleigh	Colorado	
51						

Adjusting Common Page Setup Settings

Clicking the Quick Print button (or choosing File ➪ Print ➪ Print) may produce acceptable results in many cases, but a little tweaking of the print settings can often improve your printed reports. You can adjust print settings in three places:

- The Print settings screen in Backstage view, displayed when you choose File ➪ Print.
- The Page Layout tab of the Ribbon.
- The Page Setup dialog box that is displayed when you click the dialog box launcher in the lower-right corner of the Page Layout ➪ The Page Setup group on the Ribbon. You can also access the Page Setup dialog box from the Print settings screen in Backstage view.

Table 13.1 summarizes the locations where you can make various types of print-related adjustments in Excel.

TABLE 13.1 Where to change printer settings

Setting	Print settings screen	Page layout tab of Ribbon	Page Setup dialog box
Number of copies	X		
Printer to use	X		
What to print	X		
Pages to print	X		
Specify worksheet print area		X	X
1-sided or 2-sided	X		
Collated	X		
Orientation	X	X	X
Paper size	X	X	X
Adjust margins	X	X	X
Specify manual page breaks		X	
Specify repeating rows or columns			X
Set print scaling	X	X	X
Print or hide gridlines		X	X
Print or hide row and column headings		X	X
Specify the first page number			X
Center output on page			X
Specify header/footers and options			X
Specify how to print cell notes or comments			X
Specify page order			X
Specify black-and-white output			X
Specify how to print error cells			X
Launch Printer Properties dialog box	X		X

Table 13.1 might make printing seem more complicated than it really is. The key point to remember is this: If you can't find a way to make a particular adjustment, it's probably available from the Page Setup dialog box.

Choosing Your Printer

To switch to a different printer or output device, choose File ⇨ Print, and use the drop-down control in the Printer section to select a different installed printer.

> **NOTE**
>
> To adjust printer settings, click the Printer Properties link on the Print settings screen in Backstage view to display a Properties dialog box for the selected printer. The exact dialog box that you see depends on the printer. The Properties dialog box lets you adjust printer-specific settings, such as the print quality and the paper source. In most cases, you won't have to change any of these settings, but if you're having print-related problems, you may want to check the settings.

Specifying What You Want to Print

Sometimes you may want to print only part of the worksheet rather than the entire used area. Or you may want to reprint selected pages of a report without printing all the pages. Choose File ⇨ Print and use the controls in the Settings section to specify what to print.

You have several options:

- **Print Active Sheets:** Prints the active sheet or sheets that you selected. (This option is the default.) You can select multiple sheets to print by pressing Ctrl and clicking the sheet tabs. If you select multiple sheets, Excel begins printing each sheet on a new page.
- **Print Entire Workbook:** Prints every sheet in the workbook, including chart sheets.
- **Print Selection:** Prints only the range that you selected before choosing File ⇨ Print.
- **Print Selected Chart:** Appears only if a chart is selected. If this option is chosen, only the chart will be printed.
- **Print Selected Table:** Appears only if the active cell is within a table (created by choosing Insert ⇨ Tables ⇨ Table) when the Print settings screen is displayed. If this option is chosen, only the table will be printed.

> **TIP**
>
> You can also choose Page Layout ⇨ Page Setup ⇨ Print Area ⇨ Set Print Area to specify the range(s) to print. Before you choose this command, select the range(s) that you want to print. To clear the print area, choose Page Layout ⇨ Page Setup ⇨ Print Area ⇨ Clear Print Area. To override the print area, select Ignore Print Area in the list of Print What options.

> **NOTE**
>
> The print area does not have to be a single range. You can select multiple areas before you set the print area. Each area will print on a separate page.

If your printed output uses multiple pages, you can select which pages to print by indicating the number of the first and last pages to print by using Pages controls in the Settings section. You can either use the spinner controls or type the page numbers in the text boxes.

Changing Page Orientation

Page orientation refers to the way output is printed on the page. Choose Page Layout ⇨ Page Setup ⇨ Orientation ⇨ Portrait to print tall pages (the default) or Page Layout ⇨ Page Setup ⇨ Orientation ⇨ Landscape to print wide pages. Landscape orientation is useful when you have a wide range that doesn't fit on a vertically oriented page.

If you change the orientation, the onscreen page breaks adjust automatically to accommodate the new paper orientation.

Page orientation settings are also available when you choose File ⇨ Print.

Specifying Paper Size

Choose Page Layout ⇨ Page Setup ⇨ Size to specify the paper size you're using. The paper size settings are also available when you choose File ⇨ Print.

NOTE

Even though Excel displays a variety of paper sizes, your printer may not be capable of using all of them.

Printing Multiple Copies of a Report

Use the Copies control at the top of the Print tab in Backstage view to specify the number of copies to print. Just enter the number of copies you want and then click Print.

TIP

If you're printing multiple copies of a report, make sure that the Collated option is selected so that Excel prints the pages in order for each set of output. If you're printing only one page, Excel ignores the Collated setting.

Adjusting the Page Margins

Margins are the unprinted areas along the sides, top, and bottom of a printed page. Excel provides four "quick margin" settings; you can also specify the exact margin size you require. All printed pages have the same margins. You can't specify different margins for different pages.

In Page Layout view, a ruler is displayed above the column headers and to the left of the row headers. Use your mouse to drag the margins in the ruler. Excel adjusts the page display immediately. Use the horizontal ruler to adjust the left and right margins and use the vertical ruler to adjust the top and bottom margins.

From the Page Layout ⇨ Page Setup ⇨ Margins drop-down list, you can select Normal, Wide, Narrow, or the Last Custom Setting if you previously customized the margins. These options are also available when you choose File ⇨ Print. If none of these settings does the job, choose Custom Margins to display the Margins tab of the Page Setup dialog box, as shown in Figure 13.4.

FIGURE 13.4

The Margins tab of the Page Setup dialog box

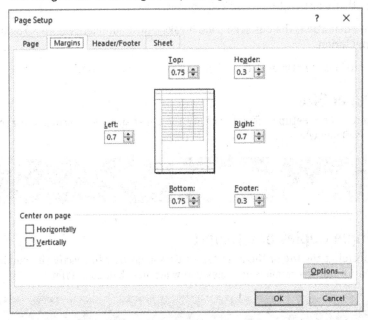

To change a margin, click the appropriate spinner (or you can enter a value directly). The margin settings that you specify in the Page Setup dialog box will then be available in the Page Layout ⇨ Page Setup ⇨ Margins drop-down list, referred to as Last Custom Setting.

> **NOTE**
> The Preview box in the center of the Page Setup dialog box is a bit deceiving because it doesn't really show you how your changes look in relation to the page; instead, it displays a darker line to let you know which margin you're adjusting.

You can also adjust margins in the preview window in Backstage view (choose File ⇨ Print). Click the Show Margins button in the bottom-right corner to display the margins in the preview pane. Then drag the margin indicators to adjust the margins.

In addition to the page margins, you can adjust the distance of the header from the top of the page and the distance of the footer from the bottom of the page. These settings should be less than the corresponding margin; otherwise, the header or footer may overlap with the printed output.

By default, Excel aligns the printed page at the top and left margins. If you want the output to be centered vertically or horizontally, select the appropriate option in the Center On Page section of the Margins tab.

Understanding Page Breaks

When printing lengthy reports, controlling where pages break is often important. For example, you probably don't want a row to print on a page by itself, nor do you want a table header row to be the last line on a page. Fortunately, Excel gives you precise control over page breaks.

Excel handles page breaks automatically, but sometimes you may want to force a page break—either a vertical or a horizontal one—so that the report prints the way you want. For example, if your worksheet consists of several distinct sections, you may want to print each section on a separate sheet of paper.

Inserting a Page Break

To insert a horizontal page break line, select the cell that will begin the new page. Make sure you select a cell in column A, though; otherwise, you'll insert a vertical page break and a horizontal page break. For example, if you want row 14 to be the first row of a new page, select cell A14. Then choose Page Layout ➪ Page Setup ➪ Breaks ➪ Insert Page Break.

13

> **NOTE**
>
> Page breaks are visualized differently, depending on which view mode you're using. (See "Changing Your Page View" earlier in this chapter.)

To insert a vertical page break line, select the cell that will begin the new page. In this case, though, make sure to select a cell in row 1. Choose Page Layout ➪ Page Setup ➪ Breaks ➪ Insert Page Break to create the page break.

Removing Manual Page Breaks

To remove a page break that you've added, select a cell in the first row beneath (or the first column to the right of) the manual page break and then choose Page Layout ➪ Page Setup ➪ Breaks ➪ Remove Page Break.

To remove all manual page breaks in the worksheet, choose Page Layout ➪ Page Setup ➪ Breaks ➪ Reset All Page Breaks.

Printing Row and Column Titles

If your worksheet is set up with titles in the first row and descriptive names in the first column, it can be difficult to identify data that appears on printed pages where those titles don't appear. To resolve this problem, you can choose to print selected rows or columns as titles on each page of the printout.

Row and column titles serve pretty much the same purpose on a printout as frozen panes do in navigating within a worksheet. Keep in mind, however, that these features are independent of each other. In other words, freezing panes doesn't affect the printed output.

> **CAUTION**
>
> Don't confuse print titles with headers; these are two different concepts. Headers appear at the top of each page and contain information such as the worksheet name, date, or page number. Row and column titles describe the data being printed, such as field names in a database table or list.

You can specify rows to repeat at the top of every printed page or columns to repeat at the left of every printed page. To do so, choose Page Layout ⇨ Page Setup ⇨ Print Titles. Excel displays the Sheet tab of the Page Setup dialog box, as shown in Figure 13.5.

FIGURE 13.5

Use the Sheet tab of the Page Setup dialog box to specify rows or columns that will appear on each printed page.

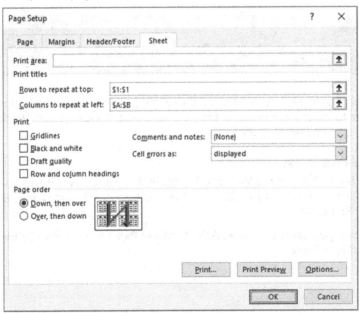

Figure 13.5 shows that row 1 will repeat at the top of the page and columns A and B will repeat on the left of the page. Even if you only want one row or column, you have to include the colon. To set these properties, activate the appropriate box (either Rows To Repeat At Top or Columns To Repeat At Left) and then select the rows or columns in the worksheet. Or you can enter these references manually. For example, to specify rows 1 and 2 as repeating rows, enter **1:2**.

> **NOTE**
>
> When you specify row and column titles and use Page Layout view, these titles will repeat on every page (just as when the document is printed). However, the cells used in the title can be selected only on the page in which they first appear.

Scaling Printed Output

In some cases, you may need to force your printed output to fit on a specific number of pages. You can do so by enlarging or reducing the size. To enter a scaling factor, choose Page Layout ⇨ Scale To Fit ⇨ Scale. You can scale the output from 10% up to 400%. To return to normal scaling, enter **100%**.

To force Excel to print using a specific number of pages, choose Page Layout ⇨ Scale To Fit ⇨ Width and Page Layout ⇨ Scale To Fit ⇨ Height. When you change either one of these settings, the corresponding scale factor is displayed in the Scale control.

> **CAUTION**
>
> Excel doesn't ensure legibility. It will gladly scale your output to be so small that no one can read it.

13

Printing Cell Gridlines

Typically, cell gridlines aren't printed. If you want your printout to include the gridlines, choose Page Layout ⇨ Sheet Options ⇨ Gridlines ⇨ Print.

Alternatively, you can insert borders around some cells to simulate gridlines. Change the border color to White, Background 1, 25% Darker to get a pretty good simulation of a gridline. To change the color, choose Home ⇨ Font ⇨ Borders ⇨ More Borders. Make sure you change the color before you apply the border.

 See Chapter 9, "Formatting Worksheets," for information about borders.

Printing Row and Column Headers

By default, row and column headers for a worksheet are not printed. If you want your printout to include these items, choose Page Layout ⇨ Sheet Options ⇨ Headings ⇨ Print.

Using a Background Image

Would you like to have a background image on your printouts? Unfortunately, you can't. You may have noticed the Page Layout ⇨ Page Setup ⇨ Background command. This button displays a dialog box that lets you select an image to display as a background. Placing this control among the other print-related commands is misleading. Background images placed on a worksheet are never printed.

TIP

In lieu of a true background image, you can insert WordArt, a shape, or a picture on your worksheet and then adjust its transparency. Then copy the image to all printed pages. Alternatively, you can insert an object in a page header or footer. (See the sidebar "Inserting a Watermark.")

Inserting a Watermark

A watermark is an image (or text) that appears on each printed page. A watermark can be a faint company logo or a word such as DRAFT. Excel doesn't have an official command to print a watermark, but you can add a watermark by inserting a picture in the page header or footer. Here's how:

1. **Locate an image on your hard drive that you want to use for the watermark.**

2. **Choose View ⇨ Workbook Views ⇨ Page Layout View.**

3. **Click the center section of the header.**

4. **Choose Header & Footer ⇨ Header & Footer Elements ⇨ Picture.** The Insert Pictures dialog box appears.

5. **Click Browse and locate the image from step 1 (or locate a suitable image from other sources listed).**

6. **Click outside the header to see your image.**

7. **To center the image in the middle of the page, click the center section of the header and add some carriage returns before the** &[Picture] **code.** You'll need to experiment to determine the number of carriage returns required to push the image into the body of the document.

8. **If you need to adjust the image (e.g., make it lighter), click the center section of the header and then choose Header & Footer ⇨ Header & Footer Elements ⇨ Format Picture. Use the Image controls on the Picture tab of the Format Picture dialog box to adjust the image.** You may need to experiment with the settings to make sure that the worksheet text is legible.

Figure 13.6 shows an example of a header image (the word DRAFT made with SmartArt) used as a watermark. You can do a similar thing with plain text, but you don't get the same formatting controls, such as controlling the brightness and contrast.

FIGURE 13.6

A header image can be used as a watermark.

Adding a Header or a Footer to Your Reports

A header is information that appears at the top of each printed page. A footer is information that appears at the bottom of each printed page. By default, new workbooks have space for headers or footers but nothing in them.

You can specify headers and footers by using the Header/Footer tab of the Page Setup dialog box. Or you can simplify the task by switching to Page Layout view, where you can click the Add Header or Add Footer section.

> **NOTE**
>
> If you're working in Normal view, you can choose Insert ⬩ Text ⬩ Header & Footer. Excel switches to Page Layout view and activates the center section of the page header.

You can then type the information and apply any type of formatting you like. Note that headers and footers consist of three sections: left, center, and right. For example, you can create a header that prints your name at the left margin, the worksheet name centered in the header, and the page number at the right margin.

> **TIP**
>
> If you want a consistent header or footer for all your documents, create a `book.xltx` template with your headers or footers specified. A `book.xltx` template is used as the basis for new workbooks. To save a file as a template, select Excel Template (*.xltx) from the Save As Type drop-down list when saving the file.

When you activate the header or footer section in Page Layout view, the Ribbon displays a new contextual tab: Header & Footer. Use the controls on this tab to work with headers and footers.

Selecting a Predefined Header or Footer

You can choose from predefined headers or footers by using either of the two drop-down lists in the Header & Footer ➪ Header & Footer group. Notice that some items in these lists consist of multiple parts, separated by a comma. Each part goes into one of the three header or footer sections (left, center, or right). Figure 13.7 shows an example of a header that uses all three sections.

FIGURE 13.7

This three-part header is one of Excel's predefined headers.

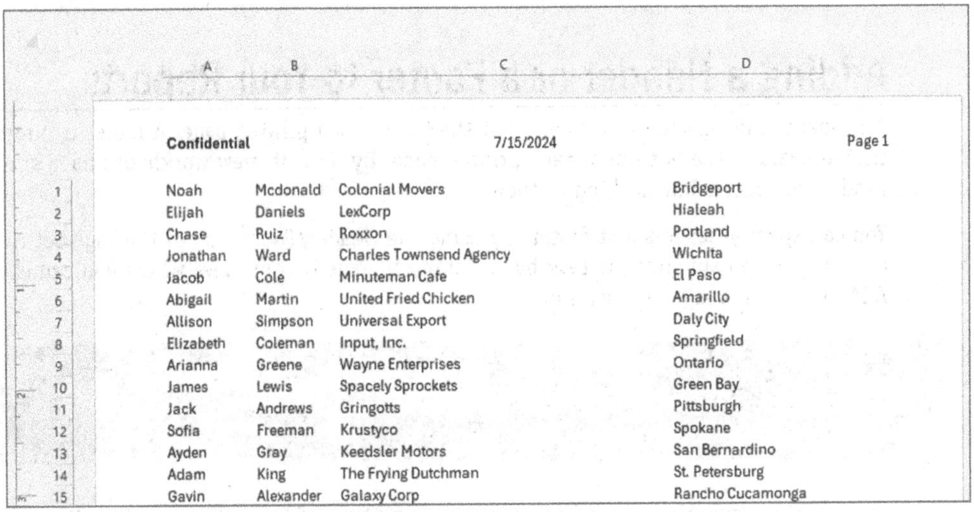

Understanding Header and Footer Element Codes

When a header or footer section is activated, you can type whatever text you like into the section. Or to insert variable information, you can insert any of several element codes by clicking a button in the Header & Footer ➪ Header & Footer Elements group. Each button inserts a code into the selected section. For example, to insert the current date, click the Current Date button. Table 13.2 lists the buttons and their functions.

TABLE 13.2 Header and footer buttons and their functions

Button	Code	Function
Page Number	&[Page]	Displays the page number
Number Of Pages	&[Pages]	Displays the total number of pages to be printed
Current Date	&[Date]	Displays the current date
Current Time	&[Time]	Displays the current time
File Path	&[Path]&[File]	Displays the workbook's complete path and filename
File Name	&[File]	Displays the workbook name
Sheet Name	&[Tab]	Displays the sheet's name
Picture	&[Picture]	Enables you to add a picture
Format Picture	Not applicable	Enables you to change an added picture's settings

You can combine text and codes and insert as many codes as you like into each section.

> **NOTE**
>
> If the text that you enter uses an ampersand (&), you must enter the ampersand twice (because Excel uses an ampersand to signal a code). For example, to enter the text Research & Development into a section of a header or footer, type **Research && Development**.

You can also use different fonts and sizes in your headers and footers. Just select the text you want to change and then use the formatting tools in the Home ⇨ Font group. Or use the controls on the Mini toolbar, which appears automatically when you select the text. If you don't change the font, Excel uses the font defined for the Normal style.

> **TIP**
>
> You can use as many lines as you like. Press Enter to force a line break for multiline headers or footers. If you use multiline headers or footers, you may need to adjust the top or bottom margin so that the text won't overlap with the worksheet data. (See "Adjusting the Page Margins," earlier in this chapter.)

Unfortunately, you can't print the contents of a specific cell in a header or footer. For example, you may want Excel to use the contents of cell A1 as part of a header. To do so, you need to enter the cell's contents manually—or write a VBA macro to perform this operation before the sheet is printed.

Exploring Other Header and Footer Options

When a header or footer is selected in Page Layout view, the Header & Footer ⇨ Options group contains controls that let you specify other options:

- **Different First Page:** If this option is selected, you can specify a different header/footer for the first printed page.

13

- **Different Odd & Even Pages:** If this option is selected, you can specify a different header/footer for odd and even pages.
- **Scale With Document:** If this option is selected, the font size in the header and footer will be sized accordingly if the document is scaled when printed. This option is enabled by default.
- **Align With Page Margins:** If this option is selected, the left header and footer will be aligned with the left margin, and the right header and footer will be aligned with the right margin. This option is enabled by default.

> **NOTE**
> If you select either Different First Page or Different Odd & Even Pages, you can no longer use the predefined headers and footers. You must use the Custom Header and Custom Footer buttons in the Page Setup dialog box.

Excel Keyboard Shortcuts

Key	Action
Workbook Operations	
`Ctrl` + `N`	Creates a new, blank workbook
`Ctrl` + `S`	Saves the current workbook
`F12`	Enables you to Save As the workbook
`Ctrl` + `O`	Opens a workbook
`Ctrl` + `W` or `Ctrl` + `F4`	Closes the current workbook
Navigation on a Sheet	
Up arrow `↑` or `⇧Shift` + `Enter`	Moves the active cell up one row
Down arrow `↓` or `Enter`	Moves the active cell down one row
Left arrow `←` or `⇧Shift` + `Tab`	Moves the active cell one column to the left
Right arrow `→` or `Tab`	Moves the active cell one column to the right
`PgUp`	Moves the active cell up one screen
`PgDn`	Moves the active cell down one screen
`Alt` + `PgDn`	Moves the active cell right one screen
`Alt` + `PgUp`	Moves the active cell left one screen
`Ctrl` + `Backspace`	Scrolls the screen so that the active cell is visible
`Ctrl` + `Home`	Moves the active cell to A1
`Ctrl` + `End`	Moves the active cell to the bottom-rightmost cell on the worksheet's used range
`Ctrl` + `←` or `→`	Selects the far left or right cell containing data in a row

Key	Action
`Ctrl` + `↑` or `↓`	Selects the uppermost or bottommost cell containing data in a column
`↑` with `Scroll Lock` on	Scrolls the screen up one row (active cell does not change)
`↓` with `Scroll Lock` on	Scrolls the screen down one row (active cell does not change)
`←` with `Scroll Lock` on	Scrolls the screen left one column (active cell does not change)
`→` with `Scroll Lock` on	Scrolls the screen right one column (active cell does not change)
`Ctrl` + `Alt` + `5`, then `Tab` as needed	Moves through floating objects such as text boxes or shapes (press **Esc** to exit)
Worksheet Actions	
`Ctrl` + `PgDn`	Moves to the next sheet
`Ctrl` + `PgUp`	Moves to the previous sheet
`⇧Shift` + `F11`	Inserts a new sheet
`Alt` + `O`, HR	Selects the name of the current sheet on the sheet **tab** for renaming
`Alt` + `E`, `M`	Opens the Move or Copy dialog box for the current sheet
`⇧Shift` + Click	Selects contiguous worksheets
`Ctrl` + Click	Selects non-contiguous worksheets
`Ctrl` + `Tab`	Activates next workbook file
`Ctrl` + `⇧Shift` + `Tab`	Activates previous workbook file
`Ctrl` + `9`	Hide selected rows
`Ctrl` + `⇧Shift` + `9`	Unhide rows in selection

Key	Action
Making Other Selections	
`⇧Shift` + arrow keys	Extends the current selection in the direction of the arrow
`⇧Shift` + `Spacebar`	Selects the entire row
`Ctrl` + `Spacebar`	Selects the entire column
`Ctrl` + `A`	Selects all the cells on the current sheet
`Ctrl` + `⇧Shift` + `←` or `→`	Selects all cells between the current cell and the far left or right cell containing data in the row
`Ctrl` + `⇧Shift` + `↑` or `↓`	Selects all cells between the current cell and the uppermost or bottommost cell containing data in a column
Formatting Selections	
`Ctrl` + `1`	Displays Format Cells dialog box or Format pane
`Ctrl` + `B`	Applies or removes bold for the selection
`Ctrl` + `I`	Applies or removes italics for the selection
`Ctrl` + `U`	Applies or removes underline for the selection
`Ctrl` + `5`	Applies or removes strikethrough for the selection
`Ctrl` + `⇧Shift` + `` ` ``	Applies the General number format
`Ctrl` + `⇧Shift` + `1`	Applies the Number number format
`Ctrl` + `⇧Shift` + `2`	Applies the Time format
`Ctrl` + `⇧Shift` + `3`	Applies the Date format
`Ctrl` + `⇧Shift` + `4`	Applies the Currency format
`Ctrl` + `⇧Shift` + `5`	Applies the Percentage format
Other Important Shortcuts	
`Enter`	Completes the current cell entry and moves one cell down
`Tab`	Completes the current cell entry and moves one cell to the right
`Esc`	Cancels operations such as editing
`F1`	Opens Help
`F2`	Enables editing for the current cell

Key	Action
`Alt`	Displays the ribbon shortcut keys (KeyTips). After pressing **Alt**, press the **tab** letter and then the command letter
`Alt` + `F4`	Closes Excel
`Ctrl` + `C`	Copies the selection
`Ctrl` + `X`	Cuts the selection
`Ctrl` + `V`	Pastes the Clipboard contents
`Ctrl` + `Z`	Undoes the previous action
`Ctrl` - `Y`	Repeats the previous action
`Alt` + `Enter`	Creates a new line in the cell when making a cell entry
`Ctrl` + `G` or `F5`	Opens the Go To dialog box
`Ctrl` + `;`	Enters the current date in the cell
`Ctrl` + `⇧Shift` + `;`	Enters the current time in the cell
`Ctrl` + `K`	Inserts a hyperlink
`Ctrl` + `F`	Begins a find operation
`Ctrl` + `H`	Begins a replace operation
`⇧Shift` + `F3`	Opens the Insert Function dialog box
`=`	Starts a formula
`F4`	Toggles between relative and absolute references in a formula
`Delete`	Deletes the contents of the selected cell
`F9`	Calculates the worksheet
`Ctrl` + `F3`	Opens the Name Manager dialog box
`F7`	Checks spelling
`Alt` + `F11`	Creates an embedded chart of the selected data
`F11`	Creates a chart sheet of the selected data
`Ctrl` + `F1`	Hides or displays the ribbon
`Ctrl` + `T`	Converts the selection to a table